# His Names Are Wonderful

*. . . The desire of all our soul is to remember you and your name.* Isaiah 26:8

## Dedication

To Beth B.
Who desired a closer walk with her Lord
and needed a tool to do so,
whose body is paralyzed,
but whose spirit is walking, leaping, and praising God.

## Acknowledgments

We will never look at a book in the same way again! After we jumped into the deep water with this one, we were helped by Mike Lohrberg, our Hebrew teacher, and Vicki Tasman, our photographer/researcher/encourager. We are very grateful for the patience and help of our husbands who were totally ignored for a few months.

# His Names Are Wonderful

## Getting to Know God
## Through His HEBREW Names

Elizabeth L. Vander Meulen & Barbara D. Malda

Lederer Books
a division of
**Messianic Jewish Publishers**
Clarksville, Maryland

Scripture quotations are taken from and follow the order, format, and numbering of the *Complete Jewish Bible*, Copyright © 1998 by David H. Stern, published by Jewish New Testament Publications, Inc. Used by permission.

10  09  08  07  06  05        6  5  4  3  2  1

ISBN-13: 978-1-880226-30-8
ISBN-10: 1-880226-30-8

Library of Congress Control Number: 2005925250
Printed in the United States of America

Lederer Books
a division of
Messianic Jewish Publishers
P.O. Box 615
Clarksville, Maryland  21029

Distributed by
Messianic Jewish Resources International
Order line: (800) 410-7367
E-mail: lederer@messianicjewish.net
Website: www.messianicjewish.net

*About the cover:* The cover illustration has been reproduced from an original painting by Barbara D. Malda. The painting is 10' wide and 4' high. In addition to the many names of God, it features a Star of David with the words of Ephesians 2:14–16 written around the edges of the star.

Contents

PRONUNCIATION GUIDE    vi

INTRODUCTION    vii
*Daniel Juster, Th.D.*

*1* ALMIGHTY    1
*The One Who Reigns in Power*

*2* FATHER    21
*The One Who Loves Us*

*3* REDEEMER    39
*The One Who Sets Us Free*

*4* SHEPHERD    59
*The One Who Cares for Us*

*5* SPIRIT    77
*The One Who Fills and Empowers Us*

*6* TRUTH    95
*The One Who Gives Us Wisdom*

*7* DEFENDER    113
*The One Who Protects Us*

*8* FAITHFUL    131
*The One Who is Trustworthy*

INDEX OF NAMES    149

## Guide for Pronunciation of Hebrew Transliteration

An effort has been made to conform to modern Israeli pronunciation of Hebrew.
We have adhered to the pronunciation guide below,
except in cases where convention has rendered a standard spelling.

- "a" is pronounced "ah" as in "hurrah"
- "ai" is pronounced "uy" as in "buy"
- "e" is pronounced "eh" as in "get"
- "ey" is pronounced "ay" as in "day"
- "i" is pronounced "ee" as in "see"
- "u" is pronounced "oo" as in "soon"
- "kh" and "ch" have no actual English equivalent;

they are gutteral sounds, which are made in the back of the throat

## Use of the *Tanakh* in the *B'rit Hadashah*

Throughout this book, you will notice passages in bold letters.
They indicate phrases or verses in the *B'rit Hadashah* (New Testament)
that are from the *Tanakh*. The word *Tanakh* is an acronym for *Torah* (Pentateuch),
*Nevi'im* (Prophets), and *K'tuvim* (Writings), commonly known as the "Old Testament."

# Introduction

### Daniel Juster, Th.D.

Our relationship with God is the most important relationship of our life. Through this relationship, the reality of God's love, life, forgiveness, and power enter our life. As Paul wrote in Philippians 3:8, everything else pales in comparison with knowing God!

But how do we know God? We know God through his son Yeshua (Jesus). As the Scriptures clearly state, "There is salvation in no one else, for there is no other name under heaven given to mankind by whom we must be saved" (Acts 4:12). This verse speaks of the wonderful salvation offered through Yeshua. But it also gives us a clue to the sometimes mysterious process of knowing God. *For this passage clearly identifies the person Yeshua with the name Yeshua.*

How expressive of Hebrew thought! A name was not just a way of identifying a person; it was a way of revealing their very identity. It is the same with the names of God, only in the Scriptures; God's identity is expressed not in one name, but in many. Each name of God is like a curtained window. Draw back the curtain and the light will flood in, giving us glimpses of his infinite glory.

An example of this can be found in Exodus 3:13–22. Moses asks God what his "name" is. Was he just asking what he should call God? No—he was asking, "*Who* are you? Describe yourself." God's response tells us this: God doesn't just say "I'm God." He explains that he is eternal, he is the God of the Jewish people, a God of compassion who has taken notice of Israel's captivity and will free them. Moses asked for a name. He was given an expression of God's essence, his compassion, and his desire to free his people.

In Jewish tradition, the many names of God are ways to express different aspects of God's presence and activity in the world. Draw back the curtain and now we see not only his glories, but even the darker corners of life are also illumined. We can see that God is at work there, too. For example, one of the traditional names of God is *El Rachum* (Merciful God). This doesn't merely tell us something about who God is in himself, but *how he feels and acts toward us!* Even when God acts in his holiness, we can be assured that his heart is stirred with sympathy and kindness toward us.

As we read through the Bible, we come across new names and attributes of God and—if only we pause and "tarry there awhile"—we will learn something fresh and marvelous about him. But also, as we read the Scriptures, we encounter some of the same names and phrases used to describe God repeatedly. And as we draw back the curtain once again, they are filled with new and deeper meaning.

How often we read a passage such as Psalm 83:19, "You alone, whose name is ADONAI, are the Most High over all the earth" without *pausing*, without taking a few moments to meditate on the wonderful name of God mentioned in the verse (see p. 12). Let the authors help you open that curtain. These windows to God — God's many names—lie "hidden in plain sight," scattered thickly throughout God's word.

You have in your hands a valuable book of scriptural meditations on the names of God. Savor each one. These pages have the dynamic potential to change the way you think about God, the way you pray, and the way you live. *His names are wonderful!*

## About the Tetragrammaton and the Use of the Name *Adonai*

The authors have chosen not to use, what is perhaps, the most profound name of God, spelled in Hebrew *yud-hey-vav-hey*, also called the Tetragrammaton. This is considered to be the holiest name of God, reflecting God's essence in a way that no other name does. Because of its holiness, this name is no longer even pronounced by Jewish people today. We do not even know for sure *how* it would be pronounced. But the reason that a meditation on the Tetragrammaton does not appear in this book is because it would require a book all to itself, a book that would include meditation after meditation.

The same understanding applies to the name "*Adonai*," (normally translated LORD, with small capital letters, but shown in this book as "Lord"). This name only appears in this volume in conjunction with other words, such as "Lord God of the Hebrews" and "The Lord of Victory."

1

*Almighty*

*The One Who*
*Reigns in Power*

God Almighty 2

High, Exalted One 3

I Am That I Am 4

Living God 5

Holy One of Israel 6

Head Over All 7

The Greatness on High 8

King of Kings 9

God of Glory 10

Lord of All the Earth 11

God Most High 12

God in Heaven 13

Lord of Lords 14

Ruler 15

Enthroned One 16

The Lord is One 17

King of the Nations 18

True God 19

Great God 20

# GOD ALMIGHTY

*El Shaddai*     אֵל שַׁדַּי

**Genesis 17:1**

When Avram [Abram] was 99 years old
ADONAI appeared to Avram and said to him,
"I am *El Shaddai* [God Almighty]. Walk in my
presence and be pure-hearted."

**Genesis 35:10–11**

God said to him, "Your name is Ya'akov [Jacob],
but you will be called Ya'akov no longer; your
name will be Isra'el." Thus he named him Isra'el.
God further said to him, "I am *El Shaddai*. Be
fruitful and multiply. A nation, indeed a group of
nations, will come from you; kings will be
descended from you."

**Exodus 6:2–3**

. . . "I am ADONAI. I appeared to Avraham
[Abraham], Yitz'chak [Isaac] and Ya'akov as
*El Shaddai*, although I did not make myself
known to them by my name, *Yud-Heh-Vav-Heh*
[ADONAI]."

**Numbers 24:4**

". . . the speech of him who hears God's words;
who sees what *Shaddai* sees,
who has fallen, yet has open eyes."

**Job 32:8**

"But it is the spirit in a person, the breath from
*Shaddai*, that gives him understanding."

---

*Who holds the universe together? No one but God, who is infinitely superior in strength and power, knows all things, and sustains the universe. That's mighty!*

# HIGH, EXALTED ONE

Ram V'nisa 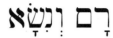 רָם וְנִשָּׂא

**Isaiah 57:14–15**

Then he will say,

> "Keep building! Keep building! Clear the way!
> Remove everything blocking my people's path!"
> For thus says the High, Exalted One
> who lives forever, whose name is Holy:
> "I live in the high and holy place
> but also with the broken and humble,
> in order to revive the spirit of the humble
> and revive the hearts of the broken ones."

**Acts 2:32–33**

"God raised up this Yeshua! And we are all witnesses of it!"

"Moreover, he has been exalted to **the right hand of God**; has received from the Father what he promised, namely, the *Ruach HaKodesh* [Holy Spirit]; and has poured out this gift, which you are both seeing and hearing."

**Philippians 2:9–11**

Therefore God raised him to the highest place and gave him the name above every name;

that in honor of the name given Yeshua,
**every knee will bow —**
in heaven, on earth and under the earth —
**and every tongue will acknowledge**
that Yeshua the Messiah is ADONAI —
to the glory of God the Father.

---

*Oh, Lord, we lift you up on high; you are elevated above all powers and principalities. We extol you, and give you the highest praise. You alone deserve our songs of joy and deep worship flowing from our hearts.*

# I Am That I Am

Ehyeh Asher Ehyeh

**Exodus 3:14**

God said to Moshe, "*Ehyeh Asher Ehyeh*
[I am/will be what I am/will be]," and added,
"Here is what to say to the people of Isra'el:
'*Ehyeh* [I Am *or* I Will Be] has sent me to you.'"

**John 8:58**

Yeshua said to them, "Yes, indeed! Before
Avraham [Abraham] came into being, I AM!"

*This name encompasses all of God's other names as he declares himself to be more than we can ever comprehend—a God who was, who is, and who will always be.*

# Living God

 *Elohim Chayim*     אֱלֹהִים חַיִּים

### 1 Samuel 17:26

David said to the men standing with him, "What reward will be given to the man who kills this P'lishti [Philistine] and removes this disgrace from Isra'el? Who is this uncircumcised P'lishti anyway, that he challenges the armies of the living God?"

### Psalm 84:3

My soul yearns, yes, faints with longing
for the courtyards of ADONAI;
my heart and body cry for joy
to the living God.

### Daniel 6:21, 27

On approaching the pit where Dani'el was, the king cried in a pained voice to Dani'el, "Dani'el, servant of the living God! Has your God, whom you are always serving, been able to save you from the lions?"

"I herewith issue a decree that everywhere in my kingdom, people are to tremble and be in awe of the God of Dani'el.

"For he is the living God;
he endures forever.
His kingdom will never be destroyed;
his rulership will last till the end."

### Matthew 16:15–16

"But you . . . who do you say I am?" Shim'on Kefa [Simon Peter] answered, "You are the *Mashiach* [Messiah], the Son of the living God."

---

*What a wonderful God we have! The author of life has breathed life into every creature. He is life itself. Living God, thank you for living in me.*

# HOLY ONE OF ISRAEL

*K'dosh Yisra'el*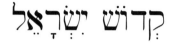

**Isaiah 12:6**
> Shout and sing for joy,
> you who live in Tziyon [Zion];
> for the Holy One of Isra'el
> is with you in his greatness!"

**Isaiah 17:7**
> On that day, a person will heed his Maker
> and turn his eyes toward the Holy One of Isra'el.

**Isaiah 29:19**
> The humble will again rejoice in ADONAI
> and the poor exult in the Holy One of Isra'el.

**Isaiah 43:14–15**
> Here is what ADONAI, your redeemer,
> the Holy One of Isra'el, says:
> "For your sake I have sent [an army] to Bavel
> [Babylon] and knocked down the fleeing Kasdim
> [Chaldeans], all of them;
> their songs of triumph are now lamentations.
> I am ADONAI, your Holy One,
> the Creator of Isra'el, your King."

**Psalm 71:22**
> As for me, I will praise you with a lyre
> for your faithfulness, my God.
> I will sing praises to you with a lute,
> Holy One of Isra'el.

---

*God, you alone are holy. Awesome God, creator of your people Isra'el, you alone are worthy of our worship and praise.*

# Head Over All

*L'khol L'rosh* 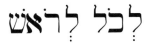 לְכֹל לְרֹאשׁ

### 1 Chronicles 29:11–12

"Yours, ADONAI, is the greatness, the power, the glory, the victory and the majesty; for everything in heaven and on earth is yours. The kingdom is yours, ADONAI; and you are exalted as head over all. Riches and honor come from you, you rule everything, in your hand is power and strength, you have the capacity to make great and to give strength to all."

### Ephesians 1:22–23

Also, he has **put all things under his feet** and made him head over everything for the Messianic Community, which is his body, the full expression of him who fills all creation.

---

*God, you are our exalted leader and ruler. You are subject to none. You are worthy of all honor. We submit to your authority and give you first place in our lives.*

# THE GREATNESS ON HIGH

## HaG'dulah BaM'romim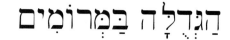

### Deuteronomy 3:24
"'Adonai ELOHIM, you have begun to reveal your greatness to your servant, and your strong hand — for what other god is there in heaven or on earth that can do the works and mighty deeds that you do?'"

### Psalm 34:4
Proclaim with me the greatness of ADONAI; let us exalt his name together.

### Psalm 104:1
Bless ADONAI, my soul! ADONAI, my God, you are very great; you are clothed with glory and majesty.

### Psalm 145:3
Great is ADONAI and greatly to be praised; his greatness is beyond all searching out.

### Hebrews 1:3
This Son is the radiance of the *Sh'khinah* [Divine Presence], the very expression of God's essence, upholding all that exists by his powerful word; and after he had, through himself, made purification for sins, he **sat down at the right hand** of *HaG'dulah BaM'romim*.

---

*When I focus in on God's splendor, sovereignty, glory, and vastness, the things of this world grow dim and loose their grasp on me. Let us always be mindful to proclaim the greatness of our God.*

# KING OF KINGS

Melekh HaM'lakhim  מֶלֶךְ הַמְּלָכִים

**Psalm 93:1–2**

ADONAI is king, robed in majesty;
ADONAI is robed, girded with strength.
The world is well established;
it cannot be moved.
Your throne was established long ago;
you have existed forever.

**1 Timothy 6:15–16**

His appearing will be brought about in its
own time by the blessed and sole Sovereign,
who is King of kings and Lord of lords,
who alone is immortal, who dwells in
unapproachable light that no human being has
ever seen or can see — to him be honor and
eternal power. *Amen.*

**Revelation 19:16**

And on his robe and on his thigh he has a
name written:

KING OF KINGS
AND
LORD OF LORDS.

---

*Presidents, dictators, and kings rule over their nations. Our king is greater than all of these. To him all*
*power and authority belong, and all knees shall bow.*

# GOD OF GLORY

 El HaKaved  אֵל הַכָּבוֹד

**Isaiah 40:5**
"Then the glory of ADONAI will be revealed;
all humankind together will see it,
for the mouth of ADONAI has spoken."

**Psalm 19:2**
The heavens declare the glory of God,
the dome of the sky speaks the work of
his hands.

**2 Chronicles 5:13–14**
. . . then, when the trumpeters and singers were
playing in concord, to be heard harmoniously
praising and thanking ADONAI, and they lifted
their voices together with the trumpets, cymbals
and other musical instruments to praise ADONAI:
"for he is good, for his grace continues forever"
— then, the house, the house of ADONAI, was
filled with a cloud; so that because of the cloud,
the *cohanim* [priests] could not stand up to
perform their service; for the glory of ADONAI
filled the house of God.

**Revelation 19:1**
After these things, I heard what sounded like the
roar of a huge crowd in heaven, shouting,

"*Halleluyah*!
The victory, the glory, the power of our God!"

---

*In days of old, the glory of God appeared in the cloud and as a raging fire on the mountain. And just as
his glory filled the temple, it also appears through us who believe today.*

# LORD OF ALL THE EARTH

*Adon Kol Ha'Aretz*  אֲדוֹן כָּל הָאָרֶץ

### Joshua 3:11, 13

". . . the ark for the covenant of the Lord of all the earth is going on ahead of you across the Yarden [Jordan]."

"As soon as the *cohanim* [priests] carrying the ark of ADONAI, the Lord of all the earth, put the soles of their feet in the water of the Yarden, the water of the Yarden will be cut off upstream and stand piled up like an embankment."

### Isaiah 45:12

"I am the one who made the earth!
I created human beings on it!
I — my hands — stretched out the heavens,
and directed all their number."

### Psalm 24:1

The earth is ADONAI's, with all that is in it,
the world and those who live there.

### Psalm 97:4–5

His flashes of lightning light up the world;
the earth sees it and trembles.
The mountains melt like wax at the presence
of ADONAI,
at the presence of the Lord of all the earth.

---

*All we have has been given to us, but it isn't ours. It belongs to our God who made it. We care for it on his behalf. Therefore, serve him with gladness and thank him for his good gifts.*

# GOD MOST HIGH

*El Elyon*  אֵל עֶלְיוֹן

**Genesis 14:19–20**

. . . so he blessed him with these words:

"Blessed be Avram [Abram] by *El 'Elyon*,
maker of heaven of earth;
and blessed be *El 'Elyon*,
who handed your enemies over to you."

**Psalm 50:14**

Offer thanksgiving as your sacrifice to God,
pay your vows to the Most High.

**Psalm 57:3**

I call to God, the Most high,
to God, who is accomplishing his purpose for me.

**Psalm 83:19**

Let them know that you alone,
whose name is ADONAI,
are the Most High over all the earth.

**Psalm 91:9**

For you have made ADONAI, the Most High,
who is my refuge, your dwelling-place.

**Daniel 3:32**

"I am pleased to recount the signs and
wonders which the Most High God has done
for me."

---

*There is none like you, O Lord, among the gods. There is nothing higher or greater than you in all the earth. May we confess with our mouths, and acknowledge before all people, that you alone are God.*

# GOD IN HEAVEN

## Elohim BaShamayim

### Deuteronomy 4:39

". . . know today, and establish it in your heart, that ADONAI is God in heaven above and on earth below — there is no other."

### Psalm 115:2–3

Why should the nations ask,
"Where is their God?"
Our God is in heaven;
he does whatever pleases him.

### Job 22:12

"Isn't God in the heights of heaven, looking [down even] on the highest stars?"

### Daniel 2:28

"But there is a God in heaven who unlocks mysteries . . ."

### 2 Chronicles 20:6

. . . he said, "ADONAI, God of our ancestors, you alone are God in heaven. You rule all the kingdoms of the nations. In your hand are power and strength, so that no one can withstand you."

### Mark 16:19

So then, after he had spoken to them, the Lord Yeshua was taken up into heaven and **sat at the right hand of God.**

---

*Though God lives in heaven, it cannot contain him for he is everywhere, even in our hearts.*

# LORD OF LORDS

*Adoney Ha'Adonim*  אֲדֹנֵי הָאֲדֹנִים

**Deuteronomy 10:17**

"For ADONAI your God is God of gods and Lord of lords, the great, mighty and awesome God, who has no favorites and accepts no bribes."

**Psalm 8:2**

ADONAI! Our Lord! How glorious is your name throughout the earth! The fame of your majesty spreads even above the heavens!

**Psalm 135:5**

I know that ADONAI is great, that our Lord is above all gods.

**Psalm 136:1–3**

Give thanks to ADONAI, for he is good, for his grace continues forever. Give thanks to the God of gods, for his grace continues forever. Give thanks to the Lord of lords, for his grace continues forever.

**Revelation 17:14**

"They will go to war against the Lamb, but the Lamb will defeat them, because he is Lord of lords, and King of kings, and those who are called, chosen and faithful will overcome along with him."

---

*Our God is Lord of lords; there is no other master. His grace continues forever. He has come and he will come again.*

# RULER

 Moshel מוֹשֵׁל

### Micah 5:1
But you, Beit-Lechem [Bethlehem] near Efrat
[Ephrathah], so small among the clans of
Y'hudah [Judah],
out of you will come forth to me
the future ruler of Isra'el,
whose origins are far in the past,
back in ancient times.

### Psalm 59:14
Finish them off in wrath,
finish them off, put an end to them,
and let them know to the ends of the earth
that God is Ruler in Ya'akov [Jacob].

### 1 Chronicles 29:12–13
"Riches and honor come from you, you rule
everything, in your hand is power and strength,
you have the capacity to make great and to give
strength to all. Therefore, our God, we thank
you and praise your glorious name."

---

*God has exalted Yeshua at his right hand and he rules over all creation. He exercises supreme authority
over us, and governs every situation of our lives with power and strength. We are in good hands.*

# ENTHRONED ONE

Yoshev       יֹשֵׁב

### 1 Kings 22:19
". . . I saw ADONAI sitting on his throne with the whole army of heaven standing by him on his right and on his left."

### Isaiah 6:1
In the year of King 'Uziyahu's [Uzziah's] death I saw *Adonai* sitting on a high, lofty throne! The hem of his robe filled the temple.

### Psalm 22:4
Nevertheless, you are holy,
enthroned on the praises of Isra'el.

### Revelation 4:2–3, 9–10
. . . and there before me in heaven stood a throne, and on the throne Someone was sitting. The One sitting there gleamed like diamonds and rubies, and a rainbow shining like emerald encircled the throne.

And whenever the living beings give glory, honor and thanks to the One sitting on the throne, to the One who lives forever and ever, the twenty-four elders fall down before the One sitting on the throne, who lives forever and ever, and worship him. . . .

---

*When we come before the one who is sitting on the throne in all of his glory and majesty, and we see him face to face, we will fall down before him and worship him. For who can stand before the Lord our God?*

# THE LORD IS ONE

*Adonai Echad*

**Deuteronomy 6:4–5**

"*Sh'ma, Yisra'el!* ADONAI *Eloheinu,* ADONAI *echad* [Hear, Isra'el! ADONAI our God, ADONAI is one]; and you are to love ADONAI your God with all your heart, all your being and all your resources."

**Mark 12:28–30**

One of the *Torah*-teachers* came up and heard them engaged in this discussion. Seeing that Yeshua answered them well, he asked him,

"Which is the most important *mitzvah* [commandment] of them all?" Yeshua answered, "The most important is,

'*Sh'ma Yisra'el,* ADONAI *Eloheinu,* ADONAI *echad* [Hear, O Isra'el, the Lord our God, the Lord is one], and you are to love ADONAI your God with all your heart, with all your soul, with all your understanding and with all your strength.'"

*scribes, instructors of *Torah* ("teaching")

*Lord, there is no other God besides you. Only you are my God, and you are all I need.*

# KING OF THE NATIONS

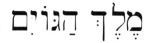

Melekh HaGoyim     מֶלֶךְ הַגּוֹיִם

**Jeremiah 10:6–7**

There is no one like you, ADONAI!
You are great, and your name is great and mighty.
Who would not fear you, king of the nations?
For it is your due! —
since among all the wise of the nations
and among all their royalty,
there is no one like you.

**Psalm 22:29**

For the kingdom belongs to ADONAI,
and he rules the nations.

**Revelation 15:2–4**

I saw what looked like a sea of glass mixed with
fire. Those defeating the beast, its image and the
number of its name were standing by the sea of
glass, holding harps which God had given them.
They were singing the song of Moshe [Moses],
the servant of God, and the song of the Lamb:

"Great and wonderful are the things you have
done, ADONAI, **God of heaven's armies!**
Just and true are your ways,
king of the nations!
ADONAI, who will not fear and glorify your
name? because you alone are holy.
All nations will come and worship before you,
for your righteous deeds have been revealed."

*There is one ruler over all the nations, and he reigns supreme. His government is incorruptible and without equal. His kingdom includes people from every nation. What a wonderful kingdom to be a part of!*

# TRUE GOD

*Elohim Emet*

אֱלֹהִים אֱמֶת

**Jeremiah 10:10**

But ADONAI, God, is the true God,
the living God, the everlasting king.

**2 Chronicles 15:3–4**

"For a long time Isra'el was without the true
God, without a *cohen* [priest] who could teach,
and without *Torah* [teaching]. But when, in their
distress, they turned to ADONAI the God of Isra'el
and sought him, they found him."

**John 17:1–3**

After Yeshua had said these things, he looked up
toward heaven and said, "Father, the time has
come. Glorify your Son, so that the Son may
glorify you — just as you gave him authority over
all mankind, so that he might give eternal life to
all those whom you have given him. And eternal
life is this: to know you, the one true God, and
him whom you sent, Yeshua the Messiah."

---

*A time will come when someone who is not God will proclaim to be God. The only way we will recognize
this deception is by knowing the true God. My one true God, help me to recognize the idols in my life that
I let take your place.*

# GREAT GOD

*El Gadol* אֵל גָּדוֹל

**Psalm 95:3**

For ADONAI is a great God,
a great king greater than all gods.

**Nehemiah 8:6**

'Ezra blessed ADONAI, the great God; and all
the people answered, "*Amen! Amen!*" as they
lifted up their hands, bowed their heads and
fell prostrate before ADONAI with their faces
to the ground.

**2 Samuel 7:22**

"Therefore, you are great, ADONAI, God; for
there is no one like you, and there is no God
besides you — everything we have heard
confirms that."

**Titus 2:12–13**

It teaches us to renounce godlessness and worldly
pleasures, and to live self-controlled, upright and
godly lives now, in this age; while continuing to
expect the blessed fulfillment of our certain hope,
which is the appearing of the *Sh'khinah* [Divine
Presence] of our great God and the appearing of
our Deliverer, Yeshua the Messiah.

---

*Our God is eminent, without comparison, and most excellent. To worship such a great God, we need to
bring him the best of what we have and who we are.*

# 2

## *Father*

### *The One Who Loves Us*

Father        22

The Close God        23

God, My God        24

Forgiving God        25

Everlasting God        26

God Who Formed Us in the Womb        27

Creator        28

God of Compassion        29

God of Kindness        30

God of Love        31

Father of Eternity        32

Giver of the Torah        33

The Lord Who Hears        34

God Who Sees        35

The Lord Our Maker        36

God of Israel        37

The Lord Our Father        38

# FATHER

*Abba* אַבָּא

### Isaiah 63:16

. . . for you are our father.
Even if Avraham [Abraham] were not to know us,
and Isra'el were not to acknowledge us,
you, ADONAI, are our father . . .

### Matthew 6:8–10

"Don't be like them, because your Father knows
what you need before you ask him. You,
therefore, pray like this:

'Our Father in heaven!
   May your Name be kept holy.
May your Kingdom come,
   your will be done on earth as in heaven.'"

### Romans 8:14–16

All who are led by God's Spirit are God's sons.
For you did not receive a spirit of slavery to bring
you back again into fear; on the contrary, you
received the Spirit, who makes us sons and by
whose power we cry out, "*Abba!*" (that is, "Dear
Father!"). The Spirit himself bears witness with
our own spirits that we are children of God.

---

*The relationship we have with our Father is one of intimacy and familiarity, awe and respect, obedience
and delight. Our Father loves to hear us call his name. He takes great delight in us and when we are
troubled, he will quiet us with his loving arms. What a privilege it is to be a child of God!*

# THE CLOSE GOD

Elohim K'rovim

### Deuteronomy 4:7
For what great nation is there that has God as close to them as ADONAI our God is, whenever we call on him?

### Psalm 119:151
You are close by, ADONAI; and all your *mitzvot* [commandments] are truth.

### Psalm 145:18
ADONAI is close to all who call on him, to all who sincerely call on him.

### Philippians 4:5
Let everyone see how reasonable and gentle you are. The lord is near!

### James 4:8
Come close to God, and he will come close to you. . . .

*Have you ever felt like God is far away? In fact, he's right there by your side, every minute of every day. Draw close to him and listen for his voice.*

# GOD, MY GOD

Elohim Elohai  אֱלֹהִים אֱלֹהָי

**2 Samuel 22:7, 22–23**

"In my distress I called to ADONAI;
yes, I called to my God.
Out of his temple he heard my voice,
and my cry entered his ears."

"For I have kept the ways of ADONAI,
I have not done evil by leaving my God;
for all his rulings were before me,
I did not depart from his regulations."

**Psalm 43:4**

Then I will go to the altar of God,
to God, my joy and delight;
I will praise you on the lyre,
God, my God.

**Ruth 1:16**

But Rut [Ruth] said,

"Don't press me to leave you
and stop following you;
for wherever you go, I will go;
and wherever you stay, I will stay.
Your people will be my people
and your God will be my God."

---

*We must leave everything to follow God. Putting the past behind us, we must determine to focus on him, the One who is our supreme joy and delight.*

# FORGIVING GOD

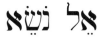 *El Nosey* אֵל נֹשֵׂא

### Micah 7:18
Who is a God like you,
pardoning the sin and overlooking the crimes
of the remnant of his heritage?
He does not retain his anger forever,
because he delights in grace.

### Psalm 99:8
ADONAI our God, you answered them.
To them you were a forgiving God,
although you took vengeance on their
wrongdoings.

### Matthew 26:28   *my Son, my blood*
"For this is my blood, which ratifies the New
Covenant, my blood shed on behalf of many, so
that they may have their sins forgiven."

### Ephesians 1:7–8
In union with him, through the shedding of his
blood, we are set free — our sins are forgiven;
this accords with the wealth of the grace he has
lavished on us. . . .

 *in union with the Fathers Son*

*Are you stuck, making one wrong choice after another, feeling trapped and condemned? Turn your heart to
our forgiving God. Repent, and you will be forgiven.*

# Everlasting God

El 'Olam     אֵל עוֹלָם

**Genesis 21:33**

Avraham planted a tamarisk tree in Be'er-Sheva [Beersheba], and there he called on the name of ADONAI, the everlasting God.

**Isaiah 40:28**

Haven't you known, haven't you heard
that the everlasting God, ADONAI,
the Creator of the ends of the earth,
does not grow tired or weary?
His understanding cannot be fathomed.

**Romans 16:25–27**

Now to God, who can strengthen you, according to my Good News,
in harmony with the revelation of the secret truth which is the proclamation of Yeshua the Messiah, kept hidden in silence for ages and ages,
but manifested now through prophetic writings, in keeping with the command of God the Eternal, and communicated to all the Gentiles
to promote in them trust-grounded obedience —
to the only wise God, through Yeshua the Messiah, be the glory forever and ever!

*Amen.*

---

*God, you are without beginning or end. You have existed through all time. You are forever the same, unchanging, infinite, boundless, without measure, and limitless. I find peace in knowing that you are my "forever" God.*

# GOD WHO FORMED US IN THE WOMB

Etzarkhah Va'Beten  אֶצָּרְךָ בַבֶּטֶן

**Jeremiah 1:5**
"Before I formed you in the womb, I knew you;
before you were born, I separated you for myself.
I have appointed you to be a prophet to the
nations."

**Psalm 139:13–16**
For you fashioned my inmost being,
you knit me together in my mother's womb.
I thank you because I am awesomely made,
wonderfully; your works are wonders —
I know this very well.

My bones were not hidden from you
when I was being made in secret,
intricately woven in the depths of the earth.
Your eyes could see me as an embryo,
but in your book all my days were already written;
my days had been shaped
before any of them existed.

---

*While you were still in your mother's womb, God was forming you into the exact person he wanted you to be. God had a plan and purpose for you before you even existed. Therefore, strive to be all that he wants you to be. Rejoice in who you are and who you will become with his help.*

# CREATOR

Berey  בּוֹרֵא

**Isaiah 43:15**
"I am ADONAI, your Holy One,
the Creator of Isra'el, your King."

**Jeremiah 33:2**
"Thus says ADONAI the maker,
ADONAI who formed [the universe]
so as to keep directing it —
ADONAI is his name . . ."

**Psalm 95:4–5**
He holds the depths of the earth in his hands;
the mountain peaks too belong to him.
The sea is his — he made it —
and his hands shaped the dry land.

**Ephesians 3:8–10**
To me, the least important of all God's holy
people, was given this privilege of announcing to
the Gentiles the Good News of the Messiah's
unfathomable riches, and of letting everyone see
how this secret plan is going to work out. This
plan, kept hidden for ages by God, the Creator
of everything, is for the rulers and authorities in
heaven to learn, through the existence of the
Messianic Community, how many-sided God's
wisdom is.

---

*The glory of God is all around us in his creation—in a golden sunrise, a beautiful pink rose, and a turquoise blue sky. Everything he made has beauty all its own. Give thanks to God, the master designer.*

# GOD OF COMPASSION

 *El Hanun*   אֵל חַנּוּן

### Exodus 34:6–7

ADONAI passed before him and proclaimed: "*YUD-HEH-VAV-HEH*!!! *Yud-Heh-Vav-Heh* [ADONAI] is God, merciful and compassionate, slow to anger, rich in grace and truth; showing grace to the thousandth generation, forgiving offenses, crimes and sins . . ."

### Joel 2:13

Tear your heart, not your garments;
and turn to ADONAI your God.
For he is merciful and compassionate,
slow to anger, rich in grace,
and willing to change his mind about disaster.

### Jonah 4:2

He prayed to ADONAI, "Now, ADONAI, didn't I say this would happen, when I was still in my own country? That's why I tried to get away to Tarshish ahead of time! I Knew you were a God who is merciful and compassionate, slow to anger and rich in grace, and that you relent from inflicting punishment."

### Matthew 9:36

When he saw the crowds, he had compassion on them because they were harried and helpless, like sheep without a shepherd.

---

*God, your deep sorrow and sympathy for my sufferings and troubles strengthen my resolve to press through. You bless me with perseverance and vigor so I can reach my goal.*

# GOD OF KINDNESS

*El Hesed* 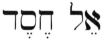 אֵל חֶסֶד

### Psalm 86:4–7

Fill your servant's heart with joy,
for to you, *Adonai*, I lift my heart.
*Adonai*, you are kind and forgiving,
full of grace toward all who call on you.
Listen, ADONAI, to my prayer;
pay attention to my pleading cry.
On the day of my trouble I am calling on you,
for you will answer me.

### 2 Samuel 2:6

"Now may ADONAI show kindness and truth to
you; and I too will show you favor because you
have done this."

### Ephesians 2:6–7

That is, God raised us up with the Messiah
Yeshua and seated us with him in heaven, in
order to exhibit in the ages to come how
infinitely rich is his grace, how great is his
kindness toward us who are united with the
Messiah Yeshua.

### Titus 3:4–5

But when the kindness and love for mankind of
God our Deliverer was revealed, he delivered us.
It was not on the ground of any righteous deeds
we had done, but on the ground of his own
mercy. . . .

*Kindness and compassion go hand in hand. When someone gives of themselves on your behalf doesn't it bless you? When someone reaches out to you in your difficulty doesn't it strengthen you? God's care for us comes through many people and in many ways. Who can you touch with his kindness today?*

# GOD OF LOVE

 *El Ahavah*    אֵל אַהֲבָה

**Deuteronomy 23:6**

"But ADONAI your God would not listen to Bil'am [Balaam]; rather, ADONAI your God turned the curse into a blessing for you; because ADONAI your God loved you."

**Romans 8:37–39**

No, in all these things we are superconquerors, through the one who has loved us. For I am convinced that neither death nor life, neither angels nor other heavenly rulers, neither what exists nor what is coming, neither powers above nor powers below, nor any other created thing will be able to separate us from the love of God which comes to us through the Messiah Yeshua, our Lord.

**1 John 4:8–10**

Those who do not love, do not know God; because God is love. Here is how God showed his love among us: God sent his only Son into the world, so that through him we might have life. Here is what love is: not that we have loved God, but that he loved us and sent his Son to be the *kapparah* [atonement] for our sins.

*Nothing can separate us from the perfect love that our God has for us. This love is unlike any other we have ever known. Because of God's great love for us, we can love others.*

# FATHER OF ETERNITY

## Avi'ad    אֲבִיעַד

**Isaiah 9:5**
> For a child is born to us,
> a son is given to us;
> dominion will rest on his shoulders,
> and he will be given the name
> Pele-Yo'etz El Gibbor
> Avi-'Ad Sar-Shalom
> [Wonder of a Counselor, Mighty God,
> Father of Eternity, Prince of Peace].

**Jeremiah 10:10**
> But ADONAI, God, is the true God,
> the living God, the everlasting king. . . .

**Psalm 41:14**
> Blessed be ADONAI the God of Isra'el
> from eternity past to eternity future.

**John 14:2–3**
> "In my Father's house are many places to live. If
> there weren't, I would have told you; because I
> am going there to prepare a place for you. Since I
> am going and preparing a place for you, I will
> return to take you with me; so that where I am,
> you may be also."

---

*Eternity, what a mind-boggling concept! It is beyond our comprehension. Our God existed before time began and we can live forever with him. Halleluyah!*

# GIVER OF THE TORAH

*Noten HaTorah*  נוֹתֵן הַתּוֹרָה

**Exodus 13:9**
"Moreover, it will serve you as a sign on your hand and as a reminder between your eyes, so that ADONAI's *Torah* [teaching] may be on your lips; because with a strong hand ADONAI brought you out of Egypt."

**Numbers 19:2**
ADONAI said to Moshe [Moses] and Aharon [Aaron], "This is the regulation from the *Torah* which ADONAI has commanded."

**Micah 4:2**
. . . For out of Tziyon [Zion] will go forth *Torah*, the word of ADONAI from Yerushalayim.*

**1 Chronicles 16:39–40**
He left Tzadok [Zadok] the *cohen* [priest] with his kinsmen before the tabernacle of ADONAI at the high place in Giv'on [Gibeon] to offer burnt offerings to ADONAI every morning and evening on the altar for burnt offerings, according to everything written in the *Torah* of ADONAI, which he gave to Isra'el.

**James 4:12**
There is but one Giver of *Torah*; he is also the Judge, with the power to deliver and to destroy. . . .

*Jerusalem

*God gave us instructions for righteous living so we could learn to follow his ways and walk in reverence before him. His teaching is perfect and true, a guide for our lives.* ⟡

# THE LORD WHO HEARS

*Adonai Yishma* 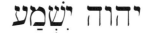 יהוה יִשְׁמַע

### Isaiah 30:19

People in Tziyon [Zion], who live in
Yerushalayim [Jerusalem],
you will weep no more.
At the sound of your cry, he will show you his
grace; on hearing it, he will answer you.

### Psalm 4:4

Understand that ADONAI sets apart
the godly person for himself;
ADONAI will hear when I call to him.

### Psalm 34:16, 18

The eyes of ADONAI watch over the righteous,
and his ears are open to their cry.

[The righteous] cried out, and ADONAI heard,
and he saved them from all their troubles.

### 1 John 5:14–15

This is the confidence we have in his presence: if
we ask anything that accords with his will, he
hears us. And if we know that he hears us —
whatever we ask — then we know that we have
what we have asked from him.

---

*Talk! Talk! Talk! We all need to be heard. We each have a contribution to make, a thought, an idea, an opinion. God knows what we are going to say even before it is on our lips. And, no matter how much we have to say, he never gets tired of listening to us!*

# GOD WHO SEES

El Ro'i      אֵל רָאִי

**Genesis 16:13**

> So she named ADONAI who had spoken with her El Ro'i [God of seeing], because she said, "Have I really seen the One who sees me [and stayed alive]?"

**Psalm 33:13–15, 18**

> ADONAI looks out from heaven;
> he sees every human being;
> from the place where he lives
> he watches everyone living on earth,
> he who fashioned the hearts of them all
> and understands all they do.
>
> But ADONAI's eyes watch over those who fear him,
> over those who wait for his grace.

---

*God sees everything that happens in our lives. In the midst of affliction, God sees us. He does not merely watch us struggle from afar; he comes to us, touches our spirits, and gives us strength to endure the trials of life.*

# THE LORD OUR MAKER

## Adonai 'Oseynu    יהוה עֹשֵׂנוּ

**Genesis 1:26, 27**

Then God said, "Let us make humankind in
our image, in the likeness of ourselves . . ."

So God created humankind in his own image;
in the image of God he created him:
male and female he created them.

**Psalm 95:6**

Come, let's bow down and worship;
let's kneel before ADONAI who made us.

**Psalm 100:3**

Be aware that ADONAI is God;
it is he who made us; and we are his,
his people, the flock in his pasture.

**Proverbs 22:2**

Rich and poor have this in common —
ADONAI made them both.

---

*All of us have been fashioned by God. The next time you are ready to find fault with yourself or others,
remember that everything God made is delightful to him, including you!*

# GOD OF ISRAEL

El Yisra'el     אֵל יִשְׂרָאֵל

**Genesis 33:18–20**

... Ya'akov [Jacob] arrived safely at the city of Sh'khem [Shechem], in Kena'an [Canaan], and set up camp near the city. From the sons of Hamor Sh'khem's father he bought for one hundred pieces of silver the parcel of land where he had pitched his tent. There he put up an altar, which he called El-Elohei-Yisra'el [God, the God of Isra'el].

**Judges 5:5**

"The mountains melted at the presence of ADONAI, at Sinai, before ADONAI the God of Isra'el."

**Psalm 68:36**

How awe-inspiring you are, God,
from your holy places,
the God of Isra'el, who gives strength
and power to the people.
Blessed be God!

**Matthew 15:31**

The people were amazed as they saw mute people speaking, crippled people cured, lame people walking and blind people seeing; and they said a *b'rakhah* [blessing] to the God of Isra'el.

---

*Awesome God, thank you for revealing yourself to your people, Isra'el. Thank you for continuing to reveal yourself to all who call upon your name.*

# THE LORD OUR FATHER

## Adonai Avinu     יהוה אָבִינוּ

**Isaiah 64:7**

But now, ADONAI, you are our father;
we are the clay, you are our potter;
and we are all the work of your hands.

**Psalm 68:6**

God in his holy dwelling,
is a father to orphans and defender of widows.

**Proverbs 3:11–12**

My son, don't despise ADONAI's discipline
or resent his reproof;
for ADONAI corrects those he loves
like a father who delights in his son.

**1 Corinthians 8:6**

. . . yet for us there is one God, the Father,
from whom all things come and for whom
we exist; and one Lord, Yeshua the Messiah,
through whom were created all things and
through whom we have our being.

**2 John 3**

Grace, mercy and *shalom* [peace] will be
with us from God the Father and from
Yeshua the Messiah, the Son of the Father,
in truth and love.

---

*God, you have cared for us, your children, as a loving father, providing discipline, direction, and encouragement. When earthly fathers fail us, you remain steadfast, molding us with your everlasting love.*

# 3

# Redeemer

## The One Who Sets Us Free

My Redeemer   40

God of My Salvation   41

Anointed One (Messiah)   42

Root   43

Man of Pains   44

Prince of Peace   45

God's Lamb   46

Our Passover   47

My Deliverer   48

Righteous Branch   49

God's Only Son   50

Great High Priest   51

Lord of the Sabbath   52

Seed of Abraham   53

Your Savior   54

God is With Us   55

The Resurrection and the Life   56

Pierced One   57

Righteous Servant   58

# MY REDEEMER

 Go'ali גֹּאֲלִי

*Isaiah 44:6*
> Thus says *ADONAI*, Isra'el's King
> and Redeemer, *ADONAI-Tzva'ot* [Lord of Hosts]:
> "I am the first, and I am the last;
> besides me there is no God."

*Isaiah 63:16*
> . . . Our Redeemer of Old is your name.

*Job 19:25*
> "But I know that my Redeemer lives . . ."

*Luke 24:21–24*
> "And we had hoped that he would be the one to
> liberate Isra'el! Besides all that, today is the third
> day since these things happened; and this
> morning, some of the women astounded us. They
> were at the tomb early and couldn't find his
> body, so they came back; but they also reported
> that they had seen a vision of angels who say he's
> alive! Some of our friends went to the tomb and
> found it exactly as the women had said, but they
> didn't see him."

*Titus 2:14*
> He gave himself up on our behalf in order to free
> us from all violation of *Torah* [teaching] and
> purify for himself a people who would be his
> own, eager to do good.

---

*Have you ever given up something of great value because of your love for someone? Yeshua gave his life for us so that we could live for him. No one loves more than our Redeemer!*

# GOD OF MY SALVATION

*Elohey Yish'i* 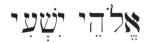 אֱלֹהֵי יִשְׁעִי

### Micah 7:7
But as for me, I will look to ADONAI,
I will wait for the God of my salvation;
my God will hear me.

### Habakkuk 3:17–18
For even if the fig tree doesn't blossom,
and no fruit is on the vines,
even if the olive tree fails to produce,
and the fields yield no food at all,
even if the sheep vanish from the sheep pen,
and there are no cows in the stalls;
still, I will rejoice in ADONAI,
I will take joy in the God of my salvation.

### Psalm 18:47
"ADONAI is alive! Blessed is my Rock! `
Exalted be the God of my salvation."

### Psalm 88:2–3
ADONAI, God of my salvation,
when I cry out to you in the night,
let my prayer come before you,
turn your ear to my cry for help!

### Luke 2:29–31
"Now, ADONAI, according to your word,
your servant is at peace as you let him go;
for I have seen with my own eyes your *yeshu'ah*
[salvation], which you prepared in the presence
of all peoples . . ."

*God, you have saved me from my enemies. You have saved me from despair and destruction. But best of all, you have provided salvation for me in Messiah Yeshua. How I praise you, God of my salvation!*

# ANOINTED ONE (MESSIAH)

*Mashiach*  מָשִׁיחַ

**1 Samuel 2:35**

"I will raise up for myself a faithful *cohen* [priest] who will do what I want and what I intend. I will make his family faithful, and he will serve in the presence of my anointed one forever."

**Psalm 132:17**

I will make a king sprout there from David's line and prepare a lamp for my anointed one.

**Daniel 9:25–26**

"Know, therefore, and discern that seven weeks [of years] will elapse between the issuing of the decree to restore and rebuild Yerushalayim [Jerusalem] until an anointed prince comes. . . . Then, after the sixty-two weeks, *Mashiach* will be cut off . . ."

**John 1:41–42**

The first thing he did was to find his brother Shim'on [Simon] and tell him, "We've found the *Mashiach*!" He took him to Yeshua. . . .

**Acts 10:37–38**

You know what has been going on throughout Y'hudah [Judah], starting from the Galil [Galilee] after the immersion that Yochanan [John] proclaimed; how God anointed Yeshua from Natzeret [Nazareth] with the *Ruach HaKodesh* [Holy Spirit] and with power; how Yeshua went about doing good and healing all the people oppressed by the Adversary, because God was with him.

---

*How marvelous are God's ways! At the exact time of God's choosing, Messiah the Prince, the Son of David was revealed. God, thank you for sending Yeshua, your anointed one, and revealing yourself to me.*

# ROOT

Sheresh  שֹׁרֶשׁ

### Isaiah 11:10

On that day the root of Yishai [Jesse],
which stands as a banner for the peoples —
the *Goyim* [nations] will seek him out,
and the place where he rests will be glorious.

### Romans 15:12

And again, Yesha'yahu [Isaiah] says,

"The root of Yishai will come,
he who arises to rule Gentiles;
Gentiles will put their hope in him."

### Revelation 5:5

One of the elders said to me, "Don't cry. Look,
the Lion of the tribe of Y'hudah [Judah], the
Root of David, has won the right to open the
scroll and its seven seals."

### Revelation 22:16

". . . I am the Root and Offspring of David, the
bright Morning Star."

---

*Just as the roots of a tree provide stability, nourishment, and a firm foundation for growth, our Messiah,*
*the Root of David, provides all this and more in our lives.*

# MAN OF PAINS

*Ish Makh'ovot*      אִישׁ מַכְאֹבוֹת

**Isaiah 53:3–5**

People despised and avoided him,
a man of pains, well acquainted with illness.
Like someone from whom people turn their
faces, he was despised; we did not value him.

In fact, it was our diseases he bore,
our pains from which he suffered;
yet we regarded him as punished,
stricken and afflicted by God.
But he was wounded because of our crimes,
crushed because of our sins;
the disciplining that makes us whole fell on him,
and by his bruises we are healed.

**Isaiah 53:11**

After this ordeal, he will see satisfaction.
"By his knowing [pain and sacrifice],
my righteous servant makes many righteous;
it is for their sins that he suffers."

**Matthew 26:36–39**

Then Yeshua went with his *talmidim* [disciples] to
a place called Gat-Sh'manim [Gethsemane] . . .
Grief and anguish came over him, and he said to
them, "My heart is so filled with sadness that I
could die! Remain here and stay awake with
me." Going on a little farther, he fell on his face,
praying, "My Father, if possible, let this cup
pass from me! Yet — not what I want, but what
you want!"

---

*With gratitude, I think of the anguish and suffering that Yeshua chose to endure for me. Therefore, in the midst of life's trials, let us eagerly say to God, "not what I want, but what you want," as he did.*

# PRINCE OF PEACE

*Sar Shalom* שַׂר־שָׁלוֹם

**Isaiah 9:5**

> For a child is born to us,
> a son is given to us;
> dominion will rest on his shoulders,
> and he will be given the name
> Pele-Yo'etz El Gibbor
> Avi-'Ad Sar-Shalom
> [Wonder of a Counselor, Mighty God,
> Father of Eternity, Prince of Peace].

**Philippians 4:6–9**

> Don't worry about anything; on the contrary,
> make your requests known to God by prayer and
> petition, with thanksgiving. Then God's *shalom*,
> passing all understanding, will keep your hearts
> and minds safe in union with the Messiah
> Yeshua. In conclusion, brothers, focus your
> thoughts on what is true, noble, righteous, pure,
> lovable or admirable, on some virtue or on
> something praiseworthy. Keep doing what you
> have learned and received from me, what you
> have heard and seen me doing; then the God
> who gives *shalom* will be with you.

**1 Thessalonains 5:23**

> May the God of *shalom* make you completely
> holy — may your entire spirit, soul and body be
> kept blameless for the coming of our Lord
> Yeshua the Messiah.

---

*"I am stressed to the max!" Have you ever made that statement? God didn't intend for us to live like that.*
*When we submit to God, his peace will rule our hearts.*

# GOD'S LAMB

*Seh Ha'Elohim*      שֵׂה הָאֱלֹהִים

### Isaiah 53:6–7

We all, like sheep, went astray;
we turned, each one, to his own way;
yet ADONAI laid on him
the guilt of all of us.
Though mistreated, he was submissive —
he did not open his mouth.
Like a lamb led to be slaughtered,
like a sheep silent before its shearers,
he did not open his mouth.

### John 1:29

The next day, Yochanan [John] saw Yeshua coming toward him and said, "Look! God's lamb! The one who is taking away the sin of the world!"

### Revelation 5:13

And I heard every creature in heaven, on earth, under the earth and on the sea — yes, everything in them — saying,

"To the One sitting on the throne
and to the Lamb
belong praise, honor, glory and power
forever and ever!"

---

*The lambs used for offerings in the tabernacle and temple were without spot or blemish. They provided atonement for the sins of the people. Thank you God, for sending Yeshua the Lamb, who took our sins on himself so we could be forgiven.*

# OUR PASSOVER

*Pischeynu*  פִּסְחֵנוּ

### Exodus 12:21–22, 26–27

Then Moshe [Moses] called for all the leaders of Isra'el and said, "Select and take lambs for your families, and slaughter the *Pesach* [Passover] lamb. Take a bunch of hyssop leaves and dip it in the blood which is in the basin, and smear it on the two sides and top of the door-frame. Then, none of you is to go out the door of his house until morning."

"When your children ask you, 'What do you mean by this ceremony?' say, 'It is the sacrifice of ADONAI's *Pesach*, because [ADONAI] passed over the houses of the people of Isra'el in Egypt, when he killed the Egyptians but spared our houses.'"

### 1 Corinthians 5:7–8

Get rid of the old *hametz* [leaven], so that you can be a new batch of dough, because in reality you are unleavened. For our *Pesach* lamb, the Messiah, has been sacrificed. So let us celebrate the *Seder\** not with leftover *hametz*, the *hametz* of wickedness and evil, but with the *matzah* [unleavened bread] of purity and truth.

\*the ceremonial evening meal which begins Passover

*In Egypt, the Israelites put the blood of a spotless lamb on the doorposts of their homes and the spirit of death passed over them. The Messiah is our Passover Lamb. Through his blood, we pass from death to life.*

# My Deliverer

*M'falti*  מְפַלְטִי

**Isaiah 43:10–11**

"You are my witnesses," says *ADONAI*,
"and my servant whom I have chosen,
so that you can know and trust me
and understand that I am he —
no god was produced before me,
nor will any be after me.
I, yes I, am *ADONAI*;
besides me there is no deliverer."

**Psalm 18:3–4**

"*ADONAI* is my Rock, my fortress and deliverer,
my God, my Rock, in whom I find shelter,
my shield, the power that saves me,
my stronghold.
I call on *ADONAI*, who is worthy of praise;
and I am saved from my enemies."

**Luke 2:11**

"This very day, in the town of David, there was
born for you a Deliverer who is the Messiah,
the Lord."

---

*Free! Free indeed! Through Yeshua, I am eternally released from the hands of my enemies, from all kinds of bondage, accusations, curses, and every sin that so easily entangles me.*

# RIGHTEOUS BRANCH

Tzemach Tzadik 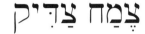 צֶמַח צַדִּיק

### Isaiah 11:1
But a branch will emerge from the trunk of Yishai [Jesse], a shoot will grow from his roots.

### Jeremiah 33:15
When those days come, at that time,
I will cause to spring up for David
a Branch of Righteousness.
He will do what is just and right in the land.

### Zechariah 6:12–13
". . . and tell him, 'ADONAI-Tzva'ot [Lord of Hosts] says: "There is coming a man whose name is Tzemach. He will sprout up from his place and rebuild the temple of ADONAI. Yes, he will rebuild the temple of ADONAI; and he will take up royal splendor, sitting and ruling from his throne. There will be a *cohen* [priest] before his throne; and they will accept each other's advice in complete harmony."'"

*Olive trees go through a season when they appear dead. But even after several years of seeming lifelessness, a branch will sprout because the roots are still alive. According to God's perfect plan, at his appointed time, Messiah, the Righteous Branch appeared, bringing new life.*

# GOD'S ONLY SON

*Ben Ha'Elohim Ha'Yachid*

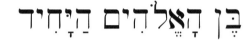

**John 1:14, 18**
> The Word became a human being and lived with
>   us, and we saw his *Sh'khinah* [Divine Presence],
> the *Sh'khinah* of the Father's only Son,
>   full of grace and truth.

**John 3:16, 18**
> "For God so loved the world that he gave his
> only and unique Son, so that everyone who trusts
> in him may have eternal life, instead of being
> utterly destroyed."

> "Those who trust in him are not judged; those
> who do not trust have been judged already, in
> that they have not trusted in the one who is
> God's only and unique Son."

**1 John 4:9**
> Here is how God showed his love among us:
> God sent his only Son into the world, so that
> through him we might have life.

---

*In times of war, many sons have given their lives for what they believe in. We call them heroes. Yeshua,
God's only son, is the greatest hero. He willingly gave his life as a ransom—not just for a country but for
the whole world.*

# GREAT HIGH PRIEST

*Kohen Rosh Gadol*     כֹּהֵן רֹאשׁ גָּדוֹל

### Leviticus 16:32–33

The *cohen* [priest] anointed and consecrated to be *cohen* in his father's place will make the atonement; he will put on the linen garments, the holy garments; he will make atonement for the Especially Holy Place; he will make atonement for the tent of meeting and the altar; and he will make atonement for the *cohanim* [priests] and for all the people of the community.

### Hebrews 4:14–15

Therefore, since we have a great *cohen gadol* [high priest] who has passed through to the highest heaven, Yeshua, the Son of God, let us hold firmly to what we acknowledge as true. For we do not have a *cohen gadol* unable to empathize with our weaknesses; since in every respect he was tempted just as we are, the only difference being that he did not sin.

*Yeshua went alone into the Holy Place as our high priest to make atonement for our sins. He became the sacrifice and he is our mediator. He dwells in the presence of God, and continually intercedes on our behalf, just as the priests did in the temple.*

# LORD OF THE SABBATH

*Adon HaShabbat*            אֲדוֹן הַשַּׁבָּת

**Genesis 2:1–3**

Thus the heavens and the earth were finished, along with everything in them. On the seventh day God was finished with his work which he had made, so he rested on the seventh day from all his work which he had made. God blessed the seventh day and separated it as holy; because on that day God rested from all his work which he had created, so that it itself could produce.

**Exodus 20:8–11**

"Remember the day, *Shabbat* [Sabbath], to set it apart for God. You have six days to labor and do all your work, but the seventh day is a *Shabbat* for *ADONAI* your God. . . . For in six days, *ADONAI* made heaven and earth, the sea and everything in them; but on the seventh day he rested. This is why *ADONAI* blessed the day, *Shabbat,* and separated it for himself."

**Ezekiel 20:12**

I gave them my *Shabbats* as a sign between me and them, so that they would know that I, *ADONAI*, am the one who makes them holy.

**Matthew 12:8**

"For the Son of Man is Lord of *Shabbat*!"

---

*God rested after six days of creating. He set the seventh day apart as holy. We can only know the meaning of Sabbath blessings when we rest as he rested. Let him speak to you about what it means to rest in him.*

# SEED OF ABRAHAM

*Zera Avraham*  זֶרַע אַבְרָהָם

### Genesis 3:15

"I will put animosity between you and the woman, and between your descendant and her descendant; he will bruise your head, and you will bruise his heel."

### Genesis 15:5

Then he brought him outside and said, "Look up at the sky, and count the stars — if you can count them! Your descendants will be that many!"

### Galatians 3:16

Now the promises were made to Avraham and to his seed. It doesn't say, "and to seeds," as if to many; on the contrary, it speaks of one — **"and to your seed"** — and this "one" is the Messiah.

### Hebrews 2:16–17

Indeed, it is obvious that he does not take hold of angels to help them; on the contrary,

**"He takes hold of the seed of Avraham."**

This is why he had to become like his brothers in every respect — so that he might become a merciful and faithful *cohen gadol* [high priest] in the service of God, making a *kapparah* [atonement] for the sins of the people.

---

*God's perfect plan was accomplished through the seed of Abraham. The seed is Messiah Yeshua, who came so that those of every tribe and nation could find life in him.*

# YOUR SAVIOR

*Moshi'ekha* מוֹשִׁיעֶךָ

**Isaiah 43:3**
    For I am ADONAI, your God,
    the Holy One of Isra'el, your Savior . . .

**Isaiah 45:21–22**
    . . . There is no other God besides me,
    a just God and a Savior;
    there is none besides me.
    Look to me, and be saved,
    all the ends of the earth! . . .

**Zephaniah 3:17**
    "ADONAI your God is right there with you,
    as a mighty savior.

He will rejoice over you and be glad,
he will be silent in his love,
he will shout over you with joy."

**Psalm 43:5**
    My soul, why are you so downcast?
    Why are you groaning inside me?
    Hope in God, since I will praise him again
    for being my Savior and God.

**Matthew 1:21**
    "She will give birth to a son, and you are to
    name him Yeshua, [which means 'ADONAI
    saves,'] because he will save his people from
    their sins."

*He is holy. We are unholy. He is pure. We are impure. He is infinite. We are finite. We have a problem. To have relationship with a holy, pure, finite God, we need a savior. Let us accept the sacrifice Yeshua made for our sins with repentance and thanksgiving.*

# God is With Us

'Imanu El      עִמָּנוּ אֵל

**Isaiah 7:14**
> Therefore *Adonai* himself
> will give you people a sign:
> the young woman will become pregnant,
> bear a son and name him 'Immanu El.

**Isaiah 8:8–10**
> . . . God is with us!
> You may make an uproar, peoples;
> but you will be shattered.
> Listen, all of you from distant lands:
> arm yourselves, but you will be shattered;

> yes, arm yourselves,
> but you will be shattered;
> devise a plan, but it will come to nothing;
> say anything you like, but it won't happen;
> because God is with us.

**Matthew 1:22–23**
> All this happened in order to fulfill what ADONAI
> had said through the prophet,
>
> **"The virgin will conceive and bear a son,**
> **and they will call him 'Immanu El."**

---

*How awesome! God came to us as a baby, born of a woman. He came, not only to be born, but also to live for, die for, and ultimately live in his people. Thank you God, for always being with us.*

# THE RESURRECTION AND THE LIFE

HaT'kumah V'HaChayim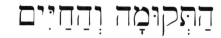

### John 5:27–29

Also he has given him authority to execute judgment, because he is the Son of Man. Don't be surprised at this; because the time is coming when all who are in the grave will hear his voice and come out — those who have done good to a resurrection of life, and those who have done evil to a resurrection of judgment.

### John 11:25–26

Yeshua said to her, "I AM the Resurrection and the Life! Whoever puts his trust in me will live, even if he dies; and everyone living and trusting in me will never die. Do you believe this?"

### Acts 4:33

With great power the emissaries continued testifying to the resurrection of the Lord Yeshua, and they were all held in high regard.

### Romans 6:5

For if we have been united with him in a death like his, we will also be united with him in a resurrection like his.

---

*On the third day after his burial, Yeshua rose from the dead. And, because he lives, we too, have the hope of resurrection and eternal life with him.*

# THE PIERCED ONE

## Asher Dakaru 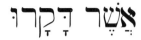 אֲשֶׁר דָּקָרוּ

**Zechariah 12:9–10**

"When that day comes, I will seek to destroy
all nations attacking Yerushalayim [Jerusalem];
and I will pour out on the house of David
and on those living in Yerushalayim
a spirit of grace and prayer;
and they will look to me, whom they pierced. . . ."

**Psalm 22:17**

Dogs are all around me,
a pack of villains closes in on me
like a lion [at] my hands and feet.*

**John 19:33–37**

. . . but when they got to Yeshua and saw that he
was already dead, they didn't break his legs.
However, one of the soldiers stabbed his side
with a spear, and at once blood and water flowed
out. The man who saw it has testified about it,
and his testimony is true. And he knows that he
tells the truth, so you too can trust. For these
things happened in order to fulfill this passage of
the *Tanakh*:

**"Not one of his bones will be broken."**

And again, another passage says,

**"They will look at him whom they have
pierced."**

*Or: "They pierced my hands and feet."

*Messiah, you paid the ultimate price for us. You bought us at the cost of being nailed to the stake and receiving the spear in your side. You were pierced for us and we belong to you.*

# RIGHTEOUS SERVANT

## Shamash Tzadik     שָׁמָשׁ צַדִּיק

**Isaiah 53:11**
. . . "By his knowing [pain and sacrifice],
my righteous servant makes many righteous;
it is for their sins that he suffers."

**Matthew 20:26–28**
"Among you, it must not be like that. On the
contrary, whoever among you wants to be a
leader must become your servant, and whoever
wants to be first must be your slave! For the Son
of Man did not come to be served, but to serve
— and to give his life as a ransom for many."

**John 13:12–14**
After he had washed their feet, taken back his
clothes and returned to the table, he said to
them, "Do you understand what I have done to
you? You call me 'Rabbi' [teacher] and 'Lord,'
and you are right, because I am. Now if I, the
Lord and Rabbi, have washed your feet, you also
should wash each other's feet."

**Philippians 2:6–7**
Though he was in the form of God,
he did not regard equality with God
something to be possessed by force.
On the contrary, he emptied himself,
in that he took the form of a slave
by becoming like human beings are. . . .

---

*If you want to become great, you must be willing to serve others. Yeshua humbled himself, taking the form
of a servant. He is our example. Ask him to help you serve as he did.*

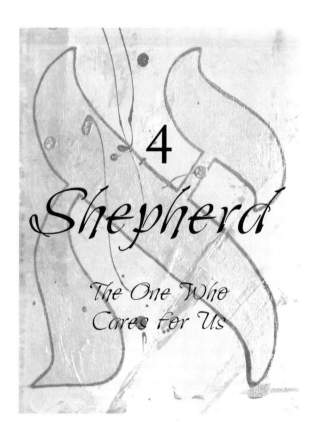

# 4

# *Shepherd*

## *The One Who Cares for Us*

Shepherd    60

Cornerstone    61

Guide    62

My Provider—The Lord Will See to It    63

Hiding Place    64

The Lord is Good    65

My Refuge    66

The Gate    67

My Helper    68

Merciful God    69

The Lord Your Healer    70

The Lord is There    71

God of My Life    72

God Who Sustains Me    73

God of All Encouragement    74

The Lord My Strength    75

God Who Carries You    76

# SHEPHERD

## Ro'eh רֹעֶה

**Genesis 48:15–16**

Then he blessed Yosef [Joseph]: "The God in whose presence my fathers Avraham [Abraham] and Yitz'chak [Isaac] lived, the God who has been my own shepherd all my life long to this day . . . bless these boys."

**Psalm 23:1**

. . . ADONAI is my shepherd; I lack nothing.

**Psalm 95:7**

For he is our God, and we are the people in his pasture, the sheep in his care.

**John 10:11**

"I am the good shepherd. The good shepherd lays down his life for the sheep."

**Hebrews 13:20**

The God of *shalom* [peace] brought up from the dead the great Shepherd of the sheep, our Lord Yeshua, by the blood of an eternal covenant.

**Revelation 7:17**

"For the Lamb at the center of the throne **will shepherd them, will lead them to springs of living water, and God will wipe every tear from their eyes.**"

---

*Sheep aren't the smartest creatures. They need someone to gather them, lead them to green pastures, and defend them against wolves. God does this for us, his sheep, and we are safe in his care.*

# CORNERSTONE

*Pinah*    פִּינָה

*Isaiah 28:16*
. . . therefore here is what *Adonai* E<small>LOHIM</small> [Lord God] says:

"Look, I am laying in Tziyon [Zion]
a tested stone, a costly cornerstone,
a firm foundation-stone;
he who trusts will not rush here and there."

*Mark 12:10–11*
"Haven't you read the passage in the *Tanakh* that says,

'**The very rock which the builders rejected has become the cornerstone!**

**This has come from** *Adonai*,
**and in our eyes it is amazing'?"**

*Ephesians 2:20–21*
You have been built on the foundation of the emissaries and the prophets, with the cornerstone being Yeshua the Messiah himself. In union with him the whole building is held together, and it is growing into a holy temple in union with the Lord.

---

*The cornerstone is fundamental to the firm foundation of a building. It marks the structure's origin and is the base for all other construction. We can rest assured that the work God is doing in our lives is secure because Yeshua is our cornerstone.*

# GUIDE

 Nocheh　　נֹחֶה

**Exodus 13:21**

ADONAI went ahead of them in a column of cloud during the daytime to lead them on their way, and at night in a column of fire to give them light; thus they could travel both by day and by night.

**Exodus 15:13**

In your love, you led the people you redeemed; in your strength, you guided them to your holy abode.

**Isaiah 58:11**

ADONAI will always guide you; he will satisfy your needs in the desert, he will renew the strength in your limbs; so that you will be like a watered garden, like a spring whose water never fails.

**Psalm 73:24**

You will guide me with your advice; and afterwards, you will receive me with honor.

**Psalm 143:10**

Teach me to do your will, because you are my God. Let your good Spirit guide me on ground that is level.

*Psalm 121*
*Adonai is your Guardian at your right hand - He will guard your life*

*When we allow the Lord to lead us, we will be successful. When we rush ahead of him, the result may be disasterous. Let the all-seeing, all-knowing God direct your paths. He is a trustworthy guide.*

# MY PROVIDER — THE LORD WILL SEE TO IT

## *Adonai Yir'eh*  יְהוָה יִרְאֶה

**Genesis 22:7–8, 14**

Yitz'chak [Isaac] spoke to Avraham [Abraham] his father: "My Father?" He answered, "Here I am, my son." He said, "I see the fire and the wood, but where is the lamb for a burnt offering?" Avraham replied, "God will provide <u>himself</u> the lamb for a burnt offering, my son"; and they both went on together.

Avraham called the place ADONAI Yir'eh [ADONAI will see (to it), ADONAI provides] — as it is said to this day, "On the mountain ADONAI is seen."

*Adonai provides salvation*

**1 Corinthians 10:13**

No temptation has seized you beyond what people normally experience, and God can be trusted not to allow you to be tempted beyond what you can bear. On the contrary, along with the temptation he will also provide the way out, so that you will be able to endure.

**1 Timothy 6:17**

As for those who do have riches in this present world, charge them not to be proud and not to let their hopes rest on the uncertainties of riches but to rest their hopes on God, who richly provides us with all things for our enjoyment.

---

*How do we determine what we really need? Sometimes we don't even know what we need or how to pray. Our Provider knows all of our needs and what is best for us, even before we tell him. Thank you God, for meeting all of my needs.*

# Hiding Place

Seter  סֵתֶר

**Psalm 17:8**
> Protect me like the pupil of your eye,
> hide me in the shadow of your wings.

**Psalm 27:5**
> For he will conceal me in his shelter
> on the day of trouble,
> he will hide me in the folds of his tent,
> he will set me high on a rock.

**Psalm 32:7**
> You are a hiding-place for me,
> you will keep me from distress;
> you will surround me
> with songs of deliverance.

**Colossians 3:3**
> For you have died, and your life is hidden with
> the Messiah in God.

---

*Have you ever gotten home from a hectic day, locked the door, pulled the shades down, and hid from life's demands and troubles, closing out the world? The next time you feel like hiding, run to God, our safe shelter in stormy times. He is the safest place to hide.*

# THE LORD IS GOOD

*Tov Adonai*    טוֹב יהוה

**Psalm 25:8**
> ADONAI is good, and he is fair;
> this is why he teaches sinners the way [to live] . . .

**Psalm 34:9**
> Taste, and see that ADONAI is good.
> How blessed are those who take refuge in him!

**Psalm 145:9**
> ADONAI is good to all;
> his compassion rests on all his creatures.

**2 Chronicles 7:3**
> All the people of Isra'el saw when the fire came down, and the glory of ADONAI was on the house; they bowed down with their faces to the ground on the flooring; prostrating themselves, they gave thanks to ADONAI, "for he is good, for his grace continues forever."

**1 Peter 2:3**
> For you have **tasted that ADONAI is good.**

---

*Chocolate fudge is delicious. But how can someone know of its goodness unless they have tasted it. Tasting produces a reaction to the flavor, texture, and richness of what we have sampled. Take time to taste and see God's goodness in your life. Count the many ways he has blessed you.*

# MY REFUGE

*Machsi*  מַחְסִי

### 2 Samuel 22:2–3

... "ADONAI is my Rock, my fortress and deliverer, the God who is my Rock, in whom I find shelter, my shield, the power that saves me, my stronghold and my refuge. . . ."

### Isaiah 4:5–6

ADONAI will create over the whole site of Mount Tziyon [Zion] and over those who assemble there a smoking cloud by day and a shining, flaming fire by night; for the Glory will be over everything like a *hupah* [wedding canopy]. A *sukkah* [booth] will give shade by day from the heat; it will also provide refuge and cover from storm and rain.

### Jeremiah 16:19

ADONAI, my strength, my fortress, my refuge in time of trouble. . . .

### Joel 4:16

... But ADONAI will be a refuge for his people, a stronghold for the people of Isra'el.

### Psalm 91:1–3

You who live in the shelter of *'Elyon* [Most High], who spend your nights in the shadow of *Shaddai* [The Almighty], who say to ADONAI, "My refuge! My fortress! My God, in whom I trust! — he will rescue you . . ."

---

*Everyday, news reports remind us of the world's troubles. Where can we hide from it all? When the cares and trials of life become too overwhelming, we can find a safe refuge in God. He is our fortress in times of trouble.*

# THE GATE

HaSha'ar     הַשַּׁעַר

**Psalm 118:19–21**

Open the gates of righteousness for me;
I will enter them and thank *Yah*.*
This is the gate of ADONAI;
the righteous can enter it.
I am thanking you because you answered me;
you became my salvation.

**John 10:1–3, 6–10**

"Yes, indeed! I tell you, the person who doesn't enter the sheep-pen through the door, but climbs in some other way, is a thief and a robber. But the one who goes in through the gate is the sheep's own shepherd. This is the one the gate-keeper admits, and the sheep hear his voice. He calls his own sheep, each one by name, and leads them out."

Yeshua used this indirect manner of speaking with them, but they didn't understand what he was talking to them about. So Yeshua said to them again, "Yes, indeed! I tell you that I am the gate for the sheep. All those who have come before me have been thieves and robbers, but the sheep didn't listen to them. I am the gate; if someone enters through me, he will be safe and will go in and out and find pasture. The thief comes only in order to steal, kill and destroy; I have come so that they may have life, life in its fullest measure."

*a name of God

*To come to God, we need to enter through the gate he has shown us. We can't go over it; we can't crawl under it or even go around it. There is only one way—through the Gate himself, and this gate is Yeshua.*

# MY HELPER

*Ezrati*       עֶזְרָתִי

**Exodus 18:4**
The name of the other was Eli'ezer [my God helps], "because the God of my father helped me by rescuing me from Pharaoh's sword."

**Isaiah 41:13**
"For I, ADONAI, your God,
say to you, as I hold your right hand,
'Have no fear; I will help you.'"

**Psalm 30:11**
"Hear me, ADONAI, and show me your favor!
ADONAI, be my helper!"

**Psalm 40:18**
But I am poor and needy;
may *Adonai* think of me.
You are my helper and rescuer;
my God, don't delay!

**Psalm 146:5**
Happy is he whose help is Ya'akov's [Jacob's] God,
whose hope is in ADONAI his God.

**Hebrews 13:6**
Therefore, we say with confidence,

**"ADONAI is my helper; I will not be afraid —
what can a human being do to me?"**

*Have you ever been in big trouble, so huge, there seems to be no way out? When we cry out in desperation for rescue, our faithful God steps in and provides a way out. He is always there, ready to come to our aid when we call upon him.*

# MERCIFUL GOD

 *El Rachum*     אֵל רַחוּם

*Isaiah 49:13*
>  Sing, heaven! Rejoice, earth!
>  Break out in song, you mountains!
>  For ADONAI is comforting his people,
>  having mercy on his own who have suffered.

*Psalm 86:15*
>  But you, *Adonai,*
>  are a merciful, compassionate God,
>  slow to anger
>  and rich in grace and truth.

*Psalm 116:5*
>  "ADONAI is merciful and righteous;
>  yes, our God is compassionate."

*Nehemiah 9:31*
>  "Even so, in your great compassion,
>  you didn't completely destroy them;
>  nor did you abandon them,
>  for you are a compassionate and merciful God."

*James 5:11*
>  Look, we regard those who persevered as
>  blessed. You have heard of the perseverance of
>  Iyov [ Job], and you know what the purpose of
>  ADONAI was, that ADONAI **is very compassionate
>  and merciful**.

---

*Thank you God, for showing us mercy when we deserve judgment. Thank you God—for lovingly meeting
us in our hour of need. There is no one who compares with you.*

# THE LORD YOUR HEALER

*Adonai Rof'ekha*  יהוה רֹפְאֶךָ

**Exodus 15:26**
>He said, "If you will listen intently to the voice of ADONAI your God, do what he considers right, pay attention to his *mitzvot* [commandments] and observe his laws, I will not afflict you with any of the diseases I brought on the Egyptians; because I am ADONAI your healer."

**Psalm 30:3**
>ADONAI my God, I cried out to you, and you provided healing for me.

**Psalm 103:3**
>He forgives all your offenses, he heals all your diseases.

**Matthew 4:24**
>Word of him spread throughout all Syria, and people brought to him all who were ill, suffering from various diseases and pains, and those held in the power of demons, and epileptics and paralytics; and he healed them.

---

*God, you are the potter and we are the clay. You fashioned our bodies and are intimately acquainted with how we are made. Thank you for caring when we are in pain. Thank you for your healing power in our lives.*

# THE LORD IS THERE

*Adonai Shamah*    יהוה שָׁמָּה

**Deuteronomy 7:21**
"You are not to be frightened of them, because ADONAI your God is there with you, a God great and fearsome."

**Isaiah 48:16**
"Come close to me, and listen to this:
since the beginning I have not spoken in secret,
since the time things began to be, I have been
there; and now *Adonai ELOHIM* [Lord God] has
sent me and his Spirit."

**Ezekiel 48:35**
"The perimeter of [the city] will be just under six [miles] long. And from that day on the name of the city will be ADONAI Shamah."

**Zephaniah 3:5, 15**
ADONAI, who is righteous, is there among them;
he never does anything wrong. . . .

ADONAI has removed the judgments against you,
he has expelled your enemy;
the king of Isra'el, ADONAI,
is right there with you.
You no longer need to fear
that anything bad will happen.

---

*Wherever I go, God is there. Whatever sticky situation I get myself into, God is there. When I am afraid and in danger, God is there. I am never, ever alone because my faithful God is always there with me.*

# GOD OF MY LIFE

El Haiyai  אֵל חַיָּי

## Psalm 42:9

By day ADONAI commands his grace,
and at night his song is with me
as a prayer to the God of my life.

## Psalm 146:2

I will praise ADONAI as long as I live.
I will sing praise to my God all my life.

## Galatians 2:20

When the Messiah was executed on the stake as
a criminal, I was too; so that my proud ego no
longer lives. But the Messiah lives in me, and
the life I now live in my body I live by the same
trusting faithfulness that the Son of God had,
who loved me and gave himself up for me.

---

*God, my life belongs to you alone. Apart from you I am nothing and have nothing. Thank you for sending Yeshua to live in me so I can live for you.*

# GOD WHO SUSTAINS ME

*El Yism'kheyni*   אֵל יִסְמָכֵנִי

**Psalm 3:6**
I lie down and sleep, then wake up again,
because ADONAI sustains me.

**Psalm 41:4**
ADONAI sustains them on their sickbed;
when they lie ill, you make them recover.

**Psalm 55:23**
Unload your burden on ADONAI,
and he will sustain you.
He will never permit
the righteous to be moved.

**Psalm 104:14–15**
. . . you grow grass for the cattle;
and for people you grow the plants they need
to bring forth bread from the earth,
wine that gladdens the human heart,
oil to make faces glow,
and food to sustain their strength.

**Psalm 146:9**
ADONAI watches over strangers,
he sustains the fatherless and widows . . .

**Psalm 147:6**
ADONAI sustains the humble
but brings the wicked down to the ground.

---

*God, you provide for all my needs and sustain my life. When I am weak and my heart is faint, you support me. Thank you for always being there for me to lean on.*

# GOD OF ALL ENCOURAGEMENT

*Elohey Kol HaNechamah*  אֱלֹהֵי כָּל הַנֶּחָמָה

**Psalm 10:17**

ADONAI, you have heard what the humble want;
you encourage them and listen to them . . .

**Romans 15:4–5**

For everything written in the past was written to
teach us, so that with the encouragement of the
*Tanakh* we might patiently hold on to our hope.
And may God, the source of encouragement and
patience, give you the same attitude among
yourselves as the Messiah Yeshua had, so that
with one accord and with one voice you may
glorify the God and Father of our Lord Yeshua
the Messiah.

**2 Corinthians 1:3–4**

Praised be God, Father of our Lord Yeshua the
Messiah, compassionate Father, God of all
encouragement and comfort; who encourages us
in all our trials, so that we can encourage others
in whatever trials they may be undergoing with
the encouragement we ourselves have received
from God.

---

*Sometimes life seems dark and full of storms. But we can weather these storms because God meets us in
our times of need through his word and Spirit. The next time you feel discouraged, go to God. He's ready
and eager to lift your spirit.*

# THE LORD MY STRENGTH

*Adonai Hizki*

### 2 Samuel 22:33–34

"God is my strength and protection;
he makes my way go straight.
He makes me swift and sure-footed as a deer
and enables me to stand on my high places."

### Psalm 140:8–9

ADONAI, *Adonai*, my saving strength,
my helmet shielding my head in battle,
ADONAI, don't grant the wicked their wishes;
make their plot fail, so they won't grow proud.

### Psalm 18:2

. . . "I love you, ADONAI, my strength!"

### Psalm 59:10, 17–18

My Strength, I will watch for you,
for God is my fortress.

But as for me, I will sing of your strength;
in the morning I will sing aloud of your grace.
For you are my fortress,
a refuge when I am in trouble.
My Strength, I will sing praises to you,
for God is my fortress, God, who gives me grace.

---

*It's easy to get overwhelmed when the circumstances of our lives are trying and our strength is depleted. But through God's strength, we can prevail against the attacks of our enemies, standing firm and full of faith. Our God gives us his fortitude when we have none of our own.*

# GOD WHO CARRIES YOU

## El Asher N'sa'akha

### Deuteronomy 1:29–31

"I answered you, 'Don't be fearful, don't be afraid of them. ADONAI your God, who is going ahead of you, will fight on your behalf, just as he accomplished all those things for you in Egypt before your eyes, and likewise in the desert, where you saw how ADONAI your God carried you, like a man carries his child, along the entire way you traveled until you arrived at this place.'"

### Isaiah 40:11

"He is like a shepherd feeding his flock,
gathering his lambs with his arm,
carrying them against his chest,
gently leading the mother sheep."

### Isaiah 46:3–4

"Listen to me, house of Ya'akov,
all who remain of the house of Isra'el:
I have borne you from birth,
carried you since the womb.
Till your old age I will be the same —
I will carry you until your hair is white.
I have made you, and I will bear you;
yes, I will carry and save you."

### Psalm 28:8–9

ADONAI is strength for [his people],
a stronghold of salvation to his anointed.
Save your people! Bless your heritage!
Shepherd them, and carry them forever!

---

*When situations cause us to feel weak and helpless, God promises not to just be with us, or near us, but to hold us next to his heart, carrying us safely in his arms all the days of our lives.*

5

*Spirit*

*The One Who*
*Fills and Empowers Us*

Holy Spirit     78

Covering     79

My Delight     80

My Joy     81

Breath of Life     82

Living Water     83

Comforter     84

My Song     85

Patient One     86

Searcher of All Hearts     87

Dwelling Place     88

Face of God—Presence     89

Spirit of the Lord     90

The Lord Who Has Anointed Me     91

Wonder of a Counselor     92

God of My Praise     93

Consuming Fire     94

# HOLY SPIRIT

## Ruach HaKodesh

**Genesis 1:2**

The earth was unformed and void, darkness was
on the face of the deep, and the Spirit of God
hovered over the surface of the water.

**Isaiah 63:11**

But then his people remembered
the days of old, the days of Moshe [Moses]:
"Where is he who brought them up from the sea
with the shepherds of his flock?
Where is he who put his Holy Spirit
right there among them?"

**Psalm 51:13**

Don't thrust me away from your presence,
don't take your *Ruach Kodesh* away from me.

**Ephesians 1:13**

Furthermore, you who heard the message of the
truth, the Good News offering you deliverance,
and put your trust in the Messiah were sealed by
him with the promised *Ruach HaKodesh*.

---

*Through the Holy Spirit, we are reminded of the truths of God's word. He helps us to pray when our
hearts are faint. And he empowers us to live righteously. Thank you God, for giving us your Holy Spirit so
we can walk in your ways.*

# COVERING

 *Kaporet* כַּפֹּרֶת

### Exodus 30:10
"Aharon [Aaron] is to make atonement on its horns once a year — with the blood of the sin offering of atonement he is to make atonement for it once a year through all your generations; it is especially holy to ADONAI."

### Hebrews 2:17
This is why he had to become like his brothers in every respect — so that he might become a merciful and faithful *cohen gadol* [high priest] in the service of God, making a *kapparah* [atonement] for the sins of the people.

### 1 John 2:1–2
My children, I am writing you these things so that you won't sin. But if anyone does sin, we have Yeshua the Messiah, the *Tzaddik* [Righteous One], who pleads our cause with the Father. Also, he is the *kapparah* for our sins — and not only for ours, but also for those of the whole world.

### 1 John 4:10
Here is what love is: not that we have loved God, but that he loved us and sent his Son to be the *kapparah* for our sins.

---

*Thank you Yeshua, for loving us so much that you became a righteous covering for us. Thank you for making a way when there was no other way. Only you cancel the debt of our sin, and we humbly receive this gracious gift from you.*

# My Delight

 *Gili*     גִּילִי

### Isaiah 58:13–14

"If you hold back your foot on *Shabbat* [Sabbath]
from pursuing your own interests on my holy day;
if you call *Shabbat* a delight,
ADONAI's holy day, worth honoring;
then honor it by not doing your usual things
or pursuing your interests or speaking about them.
If you do, you will find delight in ADONAI . . ."

### Malachi 3:1

"Look! I am sending my messenger
to clear the way before me;
and the Lord, whom you seek,
will suddenly come to his temple.

Yes, the messenger of the covenant,
in whom you take such delight —
look! Here he comes,"
says ADONAI-*Tzva'ot* [Lord of Hosts].

### Psalm 37:3–4

Trust in ADONAI, and do good;
settle in the land, and feed on faithfulness.
Then you will delight yourself in ADONAI,
and he will give you your heart's desire.

### Psalm 43:4

Then I will go to the altar of God,
to God, my joy and delight . . .

---

*Think about the things that give you the greatest pleasure in life. Is your relationship with God high on your list? Spend time today with the One who delights in you. He longs to become your delight.*

# My Joy

Simchati  שִׂמַחְתִּי

**Psalm 4:7–8**

Many ask, "Who can show us some good?"
ADONAI, lift the light of your face over us!
You have filled my heart with more joy
than all their grain and new wine.

**Psalm 105:43**

He led out his people with joy,
his chosen ones with singing.

**Nehemiah 8:9–10**

. . . For all the people had been weeping when
they heard the words of the *Torah* [teaching].
Then he said to them, "Go, eat rich food, drink
sweet drinks, and send portions to those who
can't provide for themselves; for today is
consecrated to our Lord. Don't be sad, because
the joy of ADONAI is your strength."

**1 Peter 1:8**

Without having seen him, you love him. Without
seeing him now, but trusting in him, you continue
to be full of joy that is glorious beyond words.

---

*What makes you happy? Does your heart overflow with joy when you think about God's love? Take time to think about the ways God has blessed you. And the next time you feel weak, let God's joy be your strength.*

# BREATH OF LIFE

## Nishmat Chayim    נִשְׁמַת חַיִּים

### Genesis 2:7

Then ADONAI, God, formed a person [Hebrew: adam] from the dust of the ground [Hebrew: adamah] and breathed into his nostrils the breath of life, so that he became a living being.

### Psalm 33:6

By the word of ADONAI the heavens were made, and their whole host by a breath from his mouth.

### Job 32:8

But it is the spirit in a person, the breath from *Shaddai* [The Almighty], that gives him understanding.

### Job 33:4

It is the Spirit of God that made me, the breath of *Shaddai* that gives me life.

### 2 Thessalonians 2:8

Then the one who embodies separation from *Torah* [teaching] will be revealed, the one whom the Lord Yeshua **will slay with the breath of his mouth** and destroy by the glory of his coming.

---

*We live because Almighty God has breathed life into us. By a mere breath from his mouth, the heavens were made, the earth, and everything in them, as he spoke them into existence. Thank you God, for your awesome gift of life.*

# LIVING WATER

## Mayim Hayim מַיִם חַיִּים

### Jeremiah 2:13

"For my people have committed two evils:
they have abandoned me,
the fountain of living water,
and dug themselves cisterns, broken cisterns,
that can hold no water!"

### John 4:10–11, 13–14

Yeshua answered her, "If you knew God's gift,
that is, who it is saying to you, 'Give me a drink
of water,' then you would have asked him; and
he would have given you living water."

She said to him, "Sir, you don't have a bucket,
and the well is deep; so where do you get this
'living water'?" . . . Yeshua answered, "Everyone
who drinks this water will get thirsty again, but
whoever drinks the water I will give him will
never be thirsty again! On the contrary, the water
I give him will become a spring of water inside
him, welling up into eternal life!"

### Revelation 22:17

"The Spirit and the Bride say, 'Come!' Let
anyone who hears say, 'Come!' And let anyone
who is thirsty come — let anyone who wishes,
take the water of life free of charge."

---

*Are you thirsty? Sometimes the trials of everyday life can be so draining that our spirits become dry as a
desert. Let us run to the source of living water to be revived, refreshed, and strengthened.*

# COMFORTER

 *Nochem*    נֹחֵם

### Isaiah 49:13
Sing heaven! Rejoice, earth!
Break out in song, you mountains!
For ADONAI is comforting his people,
having mercy on his own who have suffered.

### Isaiah 51:12
"I, yes I, am the one who comforts you! . . ."

### Psalm 119:75–76
I know, ADONAI, that your rulings are righteous,
that even when you humble me you are faithful.
Let your grace comfort me,
in keeping with your promise to your servant.

### John 16:7
But I tell you the truth, it is to your advantage
that I go away; for if I don't go away, the
comforting Counselor will not come to you.
However, if I do go, I will send him to you.

### 2 Corinthians 1:3
Praised be God, Father of our Lord Yeshua the
Messiah, compassionate Father, God of all
encouragement and comfort.

---

*Are you feeling sad or lonely? Are you troubled about a current problem or worried about your future? No one escapes heartache in this life. But we have a God who cares about all the details of our lives. He longs to comfort you in your suffering. Let him.*

# MY SONG

Zimrati  זִמְרָתִי

### Exodus 15:2

"Yah* is my strength and my song,
and he has become my salvation.
This is my God: I will glorify him;
my father's God: I will exalt him."

### Psalm 40:4

He put a new song in my mouth,
a song of praise to our God.
Many will look on in awe
and put their trust in ADONAI.

### Psalm 96:1–3

Sing to ADONAI a new song!
Sing to ADONAI, all the earth!
Sing to ADONAI, bless his name!
Proclaim his victory day after day!
Declare his glory among the nations,
his wonders among all peoples!

### Psalm 149:1

Halleluyah!

Sing to ADONAI a new song,
his praise in the assembly of the faithful.

---

*a name of God

*You may sing in a choir or only belt out tunes in the shower. You may have perfect pitch or wail off key. Regardless, God loves to hear you make music to him with your heart. Sing songs of praise to him today!*

# PATIENT ONE

 *Erekh Apaiyim* אֶרֶךְ אַפַּיִם

*Jeremiah 15:15*
ADONAI, you know. Remember me, think of me, and take vengeance for me on my persecutors. Because you are patient, don't banish me; know that for your sake I suffer insults.

*1 Timothy 1:16*
But this is precisely why I received mercy — so that in me, as the number one sinner, Yeshua the Messiah might demonstrate how very patient he is, as an example to those who would later come to trust in him and thereby have eternal life.

*2 Peter 3:9*
The Lord is not slow in keeping his promise, as some people think of slowness; on the contrary, he is patient with you; for it is not his purpose that anyone should be destroyed, but that everyone should turn from his sins.

---

*How LONG a 3-minute egg can take! Sometimes, it seems water takes forever to boil! We live in a society that encourages us to be impatient. Microwave ovens, fast cars, and jet planes. Yet, we have a God who is unbelievably patient and long-suffering as he waits for us to turn to him.*

# SEARCHER OF ALL HEARTS

*Khol L'vavot Deresh*     כָּל לְבָבוֹת דּוֹרֵשׁ

### Jeremiah 17:10
"I, ADONAI, search the heart;
I test inner motivations;
in order to give to everyone
what his actions and conduct deserve."

### 1 Chronicles 28:9
"As for you, Shlomo [Solomon] my son, know
the God of your father. Serve him wholeheartedly
and with desire in your being; for ADONAI
searches all hearts and understands all the
inclinations of people's thoughts. If you seek him,
he will let himself be found by you; but if you
abandon him, he will reject you forever."

### Romans 8:26–27
Similarly, the Spirit helps us in our weakness; for
we don't know how to pray the way we should.
But the Spirit himself pleads on our behalf with
groanings too deep for words; and the one who
searches hearts knows exactly what the Spirit is
thinking, because his pleadings for God's people
accord with God's will.

*In times of war, people used to use huge lights to search the darkness for enemy planes. Let God shine his searchlight on your heart to expose any darkness so you can walk in his light.*

# DWELLING PLACE

Ma'on

מָעוֹן

### Deuteronomy 12:5

"Rather, you are to come to the place where
ADONAI your God will put his name. He will
choose it from all your tribes; and you will seek
out that place, which is where he will live, and
go there."

### Deuteronomy 33:26–28

"Yeshurun [The Upright One], there is
no one like God,
riding through the heavens to help you,
riding on the clouds in his majesty.
The God of old is a dwelling-place,
with everlasting arms beneath.

He expelled the enemy before you
and he said, 'Destroy!'
So Isra'el lives in security;
the fountain of Ya'akov [Jacob] is alone
in a land of grain and new wine,
where the skies drip with dew."

### Psalm 90:1–2

. . . Adonai, you have been our dwelling place
in every generation.
Before the mountains were born,
before you had formed the earth and the world,
from eternity past to eternity future
you are God.

---

*Are you homesick? Do you sometimes feel like you don't belong anywhere? God himself is a dwelling
place for us, an everlasting abode, where we can live safely and securely all the days of our lives.*

# FACE OF GOD — PRESENCE

(*Presence*)  *P'ney Adonai*  פְּנֵי יהוה

### Exodus 33:14–16

He answered, "Set your mind at rest — my presence will go with you, after all." Moshe [Moses] replied "If your presence doesn't go with us, don't make us go on from here. For how else is it to be known that I have found favor in your sight, I and your people, other than by your going with us? That is what distinguishes us, me and your people, from all the other peoples on earth."

### Nahum 1:5

The mountains quake before him,
and the hills dissolve;
the earth collapses in his presence,
the world and everyone living in it.

### Luke 1:19

"I am Gavri'el [Gabriel]," the angel answered him, "and I stand in the presence of God. I was sent to speak to you, to give you this good news."

### Revelation 21:3

I heard a loud voice from the throne say, "See! God's *Sh'khinah* [Divine Presence] is with mankind, **and he will live with them. They will be his people, and he himself, God-with-them, will be their God.**"

---

*God, I look forward to the time when I will see your face and live in your glorious presence. Until then, may I find favor in your sight. Thank you for never leaving me alone, for being with me all my days.*

# Spirit of The Lord

Ruach Adonai    רוּחַ יְהוָה

**1 Samuel 16:13**

Sh'mu'el [Samuel] took the horn of oil and anointed him there in his brothers' presence. From that day on, the Spirit of ADONAI would fall upon David with power. . . .

**Isaiah 11:2–3**

The Spirit of ADONAI will rest on him,
the Spirit of wisdom and understanding,
the Spirit of counsel and power,
the Spirit of knowledge and fearing ADONAI —
he will be inspired by fearing ADONAI.
He will not judge by what his eyes see
or decide by what his ears hear.

**Isaiah 40:13–14**

Who has measured the Spirit of ADONAI?
Who has been his counselor, instructing him?
Whom did he consult, to gain understanding?
Who taught him how to judge,
taught him what he needed to know,
showed him how to discern?

**2 Corinthians 3:17**

Now, "ADONAI" in this text means the Spirit. And where the Spirit of ADONAI is, there is freedom.

---

*The Spirit of the Lord sets us free. Through the Spirit of the Lord, we have power to live lives pleasing to God. Thank you God, for sending your Spirit to live in me.*

# THE LORD WHO HAS ANOINTED ME

*Mashach Adonai Oti*  מָשַׁח יהוה אֹתִי

### Isaiah 61:1–2
The Spirit of *Adonai ELOHIM* [Lord God] is
upon me, because *ADONAI* has anointed me
to announce good news to the poor.
He has sent me to heal the brokenhearted;
to proclaim freedom to the captives,
to let out into light those bound in the dark;
to proclaim the year of the favor of *ADONAI*
and the day of vengeance of our God;
to comfort all who mourn.

### Psalm 23:5
You prepare a table for me,
even as my enemies watch;
you anoint my head with oil
from an overflowing cup.

### 2 Corinthians 1:21–22
Moreover, it is God who sets both us and you in
firm union with the Messiah; he has anointed us,
put his seal on us, and given us his Spirit in our
hearts as a guarantee for the future.

### 1 John 2:20
But you have received the Messiah's anointing
from *HaKadosh* [The Holy One] . . .

---

*God, you have set your seal upon us. You have anointed us and given us your Holy Spirit. Our hearts
overflow with praise. You have turned our mourning into joy and the oil of gladness fills our hearts.*

# WONDER OF A COUNSELOR

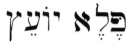

Pele Yo'etz    פֶּלֶא יוֹעֵץ

**Isaiah 9:5**
> For a child is born to us,
> a son is given to us;
> dominion will rest on his shoulders,
> and he will be given the name
> Pele-Yo'etz El Gibbor
> Avi-'Ad Sar-Shalom
> [Wonder of a Counselor, Mighty God,
> Father of Eternity, Prince of Peace].

**Psalm 16:7**
> I bless ADONAI, my counselor;
> at night my inmost being instructs me.

**Psalm 106:13**
> But soon they forgot his deeds
> and wouldn't wait for his counsel.

**John 14:15–16, 26**
> "If you love me, you will keep my commands; and I will ask the Father, and he will give you another comforting Counselor like me, the Spirit of Truth, to be with you forever."

> "But the Counselor, the *Ruach HaKodesh* [Holy Spirit], whom the Father will send in my name, will teach you everything; that is, he will remind you of everything I have said to you."

---

*Human counselors are helpful, but all truth, wisdom, and healing comes from God. For he alone understands clearly every situation. He discerns the motives of our hearts and knows what is best for us.*

# GOD OF MY PRAISE

*Elohey T'hilati*

### Deuteronomy 10:21–22

"He is your praise, and he is your God, who has done for you these great and awesome things, which you have seen with your own eyes. Your ancestors went down into Egypt with only seventy people, but now ADONAI your God has made your numbers as many as the stars in the sky!"

### Psalm 18:4

I call on ADONAI, who is worthy of praise;
and I am saved from my enemies.

### Psalm 22:24

"You who fear ADONAI, praise him!
All descendants of Ya'akov [Jacob], glorify him!
All descendants of Isra'el, stand in awe of him!"

### Psalm 150:1–6

*Halleluyah*!

Praise God in his holy place!
Praise him in the heavenly dome of his power!
Praise him for his mighty deeds!
Praise him for his surpassing greatness!

Praise him with a blast on the *shofar*! [ram's horn]
Praise him with lute and lyre!
Praise him with tambourines and dancing!
Praise him with flutes and strings!
Praise him with clanging cymbals!
Praise him with loud crashing cymbals!
Let everything that has breath praise ADONAI!

*Halleluyah*!

---

*God, I will praise you when I'm happy and life goes my way. And I will praise you in my darkest hour, in the midst of my trials, because you alone are glorious and worthy of praise.*

# CONSUMING FIRE

*Esh Okhlah* אֵשׁ אֹכְלָה

### Deuteronomy 4:23–24

"Watch out for yourselves, so that you won't forget the covenant of *ADONAI* your God, which he made with you, and make yourself a carved image, a representation of anything forbidden to you by *ADONAI* your God. For *ADONAI* your God is a consuming fire, a jealous God."

### 1 Kings 18:36–38

Then, when it came time for offering the evening offering, Eliyahu [Elijah] the prophet approached and said, "*ADONAI*, God of Avraham [Abraham], Yitz'chak [Isaac], and Isra'el, let it be known today that you are God in Isra'el, and that I am your servant, and that I have done these things at your word. Hear me, *ADONAI*, hear me, so that this people may know that you, *ADONAI*, are God, and that you are turning their hearts back to you."

Then the fire of *ADONAI* fell. It consumed the burnt offering, the wood, the stones and the dust; and it licked up the water in the trench.

### Hebrews 12:28–29

Therefore, since we have received an unshakable Kingdom, let us have grace, through which we may offer service that will please God, with reverence and fear. For indeed,

"Our **God is a consuming fire!**"

---

*Fire. It fuels the furnace that provides heat in the winter, the campfire that gives light in the wilderness, and the gas stove on which we cook our food. But it also has the power to destroy everything in its path. Let us always be mindful of the awesome power of our God.*

6

*Truth*

*The One Who Gives Us Wisdom*

Spirit of Truth  96

Him Who Knows Everything  97

The Wise God  98

Light of Israel  99

The Word  100

Light of the World  101

Living Bread  102

Spirit of Revelation  103

Refiner  104

The Way, The Truth, The Life  105

Teacher  106

Revealer of Secrets  107

Judge  108

The Lord Who Sets You Apart  109

Morning Star  110

The Real Vine  111

God of Justice  112

# SPIRIT OF TRUTH

## Ruach Ha'Emet  רוּחַ הָאֱמֶת

**Psalm 25:5**

Guide me in your truth, and teach me;
for you are the God who saves me,
my hope is in you all day long.

**John 14:15–16**

"If you love me, you will keep my commands;
and I will ask the Father, and he will give you
another comforting Counselor like me, the
Spirit of Truth, to be with you forever."

**John 15:26**

"When the Counselor comes, whom I will
send you from the Father — the Spirit of
Truth, who keeps going out from the Father
— he will testify on my behalf."

**John 16:13**

"However, when the Spirit of Truth comes, he
will guide you into all the truth; for he will
not speak on his own initiative but will say
only what he hears. He will also announce to
you the events of the future."

---

*A multitude of clamoring voices compete for our attention. Salesmen, media moguls, political pundits, and religious leaders tell us what is best. How do we know what to believe? God has given us his Spirit of Truth to lead our way. Ask him to shed his light on your path.*

# HIM WHO KNOWS EVERYTHING

### T'mim De'im  תְּמִים דֵּעִים

### Isaiah 55:8–9

"For my thoughts are not your thoughts,
and your ways are not my ways," says ADONAI.
"As high as the sky is above the earth
are my ways higher than your ways,
and my thoughts than your thoughts."

### Job 21:22

"Can anyone teach God knowledge? . . ."

### Job 37:14–16

". . . Stop, and consider God's wonders.
Do you know how God puts them in place,
how he causes lightning to flash from his cloud?
Do you know how he balances the clouds?
These are marvels of him who knows everything!"

### Romans 11:33–34

O the depth of the riches
and the wisdom and knowledge of God!
How inscrutable are his judgments!
How unsearchable are his ways!

For, 'Who has known the mind of ADONAI?
Who has been his counselor?'

### 1 Corinthians 1:25

For God's "nonsense" is wiser than humanity's
"wisdom."

And God's "weakness" is stronger than
humanity's "strength."

---

*Libraries are filled with the wisdom of man, but God's knowledge is immeasurable and cannot be contained in any amount of books. He knows the intimate details of everything—infinitely more than we can fathom.*

# THE WISE GOD

 *Elohim HeChakham* אֱלֹהִים הֶחָכָם

**1 Kings 3:28**

All Isra'el heard of the decision the king had made and held the king in awe, for they saw that God's wisdom was in him, enabling him to render justice properly.

**Psalm 104:24**

What variety there is in your works, ADONAI! How many [of them there are]! In wisdom you have made them all; the earth is full of your creations.

**Proverbs 3:19**

ADONAI by wisdom founded the earth, by understanding he established the heavens.

**Daniel 2:20**

. . . "Blessed be the name of God from eternity past to eternity future! For wisdom and power are his alone."

**Romans 16:27**

. . . to the only wise God, through Yeshua the Messiah, be the glory forever and ever!

---

*God knows best. Have you ever realized that the way God worked something out in your life was better than your own solution to a problem? Of course it was! God is pleased when we ask for wisdom. Do that so he can give you a wise and discerning heart.*

# LIGHT OF ISRAEL

*Or Yisra'el*  אוֹר יִשְׂרָאֵל

### Exodus 13:20–21
They traveled from Sukkot [Succoth] and set up camp in Etam [Etham], at the edge of the desert. ADONAI went ahead of them in a column of cloud during the daytime to lead them on their way, and at night in a column of fire to give them light; thus they could travel both by day and by night.

### Isaiah 2:5
Descendants of Ya'akov [Jacob], come! Let's live in the light of ADONAI!

### Isaiah 10:17
The light of Isra'el will become a fire and his Holy One a flame . . .

### Isaiah 60:1
"Arise, shine [Yerushalayim],*
for your light has come,
the glory of ADONAI
has risen over you."

### Revelation 21:22–24
I saw no Temple in the city, for ADONAI, God of heaven's armies, is its Temple, as is the Lamb. The city has no need for the sun or the moon to shine on it, because God's *Sh'khinah* [Divine Presence] gives it light, and its lamp is the Lamb. The nations will walk by its light, and the kings of the earth will bring their splendor into it.

*Jerusalem

*God, with your light, you led the children of Isra'el through the wilderness so they could travel during the night. Shine your light on my path so I can walk in your ways.*

# THE WORD

Ha Davar

**Deuteronomy 9:10**

Then ADONAI gave me the two stone tablets inscribed by the finger of God; and on them was written every word ADONAI had said to you from the fire on the mountain the day of the assembly.

**Deuteronomy 30:14**

"On the contrary, the word is very close to you — in your mouth, even in your heart; therefore, you can do it!"

**John 1:1–2, 14**

In the beginning was the Word,
    and the Word was with God,

and the Word was God.
    He was with God in the beginning.

The Word became a human being and lived
    with us, and we saw his *Sh'khinah* [Divine Presence], the *Sh'khinah* of the Father's only Son, full of grace and truth.

**Hebrews 1:3**

This Son is the radiance of the *Sh'khinah*, the very expression of God's essence, upholding all that exists by his powerful word . . .

---

*God, there is power in your word. Your word is just and true and gives life to all mankind. Thank you for sending Yeshua, the Living Word, so we could know you better.*

# LIGHT OF THE WORLD

## Or Ha'Olam

אוֹר הָעוֹלָם

**Psalm 18:29**
"For you, ADONAI, light my lamp;
ADONAI, my God, lights up my darkness."

**Psalm 27:1**
. . . ADONAI is my light and salvation;
whom do I need to fear?
ADONAI is the stronghold of my life;
of whom should I be afraid?

**John 1:4–5, 9**
In him was life,
and the life was the light of mankind.

The light shines in the darkness,
and the darkness has not suppressed it.

This was the true light,
which gives light to everyone entering
the world.

**John 8:12**
Yeshua spoke to them again: "I am the light of
the world; whoever follows me will never
walk in darkness but will have the light which
gives life."

---

*Streetlights, traffic lights, and neon lights cause a city to glow from a distance. But they do nothing to remove spiritual darkness. Let Yeshua illumine the dark places in your heart. He is brighter and more powerful than any electric light!*

# LIVING BREAD

*Lechem Chai*     לֶחֶם חַי

**John 6:31–35, 48–51, 58**

"Our fathers ate *man* [manna] in the desert — as it says in the *Tanakh*, 'He gave them bread from heaven to eat.'" Yeshua said to them, "Yes, indeed! I tell you it wasn't Moshe [Moses] who gave you the bread from heaven. But my Father is giving you the genuine bread from heaven; for God's bread is the one who comes down out of heaven and gives life to the world."

They said to him, "Sir, give us this bread from now on." Yeshua answered, "I am the bread which is life! Whoever comes to me will never go hungry, and whoever trusts in me will never be thirsty."

"I am the bread which is life. Your fathers ate the *man* in the desert; they died. But the bread that comes down from heaven is such that a person may eat it and not die. I am the living bread that has come down from heaven; if anyone eats this bread, he will live forever. . . ."

"So this is the bread that has come down from heaven — it is not like the bread the fathers ate; they're dead, but whoever eats this bread will live forever!"

---

*Some form of bread is used as a staple, the world over. Whether you buy it or bake it, that loaf of bread on your kitchen counter will eventually grow moldy. God gave us bread from heaven that will never spoil. Only Yeshua, the Living Bread, can satisfy our spiritual hunger.*

# SPIRIT OF REVELATION

*Ruach HeChazon*  רוּחַ הֶחָזוֹן

### 1 Samuel 9:15
The day before Sha'ul [Saul] arrived, ADONAI had given Sh'mu'el [Samuel] a revelation.

### Luke 2:30–32
". . . for I have seen with my own eyes your *yeshu'ah* [salvation],
    which you prepared in the presence of all peoples —
a light that will bring revelation to the *Goyim* [nations] and glory to your people Isra'el."

### Galatians 1:11–12
Furthermore, let me make clear to you, brothers, that the Good News as I proclaim it is not a human product; because neither did I receive it from someone else nor was I taught it — it came through a direct revelation from Yeshua the Messiah.

### Ephesians 1:16–17
. . . In my prayers I keep asking the God of our Lord Yeshua the Messiah, the glorious Father, to give you a spirit of wisdom and revelation, so that you will have full knowledge of him.

---

*A cure for cancer, a faster way to travel, a new recipe for success. All of these would be very exciting discoveries. But they pale in light of the revelation God gives us through his Spirit. Ask him to show you something new today!*

# REFINER

M'tzaref  מְצָרֵף

### Jeremiah 9:6

"Therefore," says ADONAI-*Tzva'ot* [Lord of Hosts],
"I will refine them and test them.
What else can I do with the daughter of
my people?"

### Zechariah 13:9

"That third part I will bring through the fire;
I will refine them as silver is refined,
I will test them as gold is tested.
They will call on my name,
and I will answer them.
I will say, 'This is my people'
and they will say, 'ADONAI is my God.'"

### Malachi 3:2–3

But who can endure the day when he comes?
Who can stand when he appears?
For he will be like a refiner's fire,
like the soapmaker's lye.
He will sit, testing and purifying the silver;
he will purify the sons of Levi,
refining them like gold and silver,
so that they can bring offerings to ADONAI
uprightly.

### Psalm 66:10

For you, God, have tested us,
refined us as silver is refined.

*When silver is refined, heat separates the precious metal from the dross. Too much heat harms the silver. Someone asked a silversmith how he knew when the process was complete. The silversmith replied, "When I can see my image in the silver." Be open to God's refining process and allow his image to be formed in you.*

# THE WAY, THE TRUTH, THE LIFE

*HaDerekh V'Ha'Emet V'HaChayim*

הַדֶּרֶךְ וְהָאֱמֶת וְהַחַיִּים

**Psalm 18:31**
"As for God, his way is perfect,
the word of ADONAI has been tested by fire;
he shields all who take refuge in him."

**Psalm 25:12**
Who is the person who fears ADONAI?
He will teach him the way to choose.

**Proverbs 10:29**
The way of ADONAI is a stronghold to
the upright but ruin to those who do evil.

**John 14:5–6**
T'oma [Thomas] said to him, "Lord, we don't
know where you're going; so how can we
know the way?" Yeshua said, "I AM the Way
— and the Truth and the Life; no one comes
to the Father except through me."

---

*We all like to get "there" fast. Some people like to get "there" first and always seem to know a shortcut.*
*But there are no shortcuts to God. Only one path leads to life, the one through Yeshua the Messiah.*

# TEACHER

*Moreh* מוֹרֶה

### Exodus 4:15

"You will speak to him and put the words in his mouth; and I will be with your mouth and his, teaching you both what to do."

### Deuteronomy 4:1

"Now, Isra'el, listen to the laws and rulings I am teaching you, in order to follow them, so that you will live; then you will go in and take possession of the land that ADONAI, the God of your fathers, is giving you."

### Isaiah 48:17

Thus says ADONAI, your Redeemer,
the Holy One of Isra'el:
"I am ADONAI, your God,
who teaches you for your own good,
who guides you on the path you should take."

### Job 36:22

"Look, God is exalted in his strength;
who is a teacher like him?"

### John 7:16

So Yeshua gave them an answer: "My teaching is not my own, it comes from the One who sent me."

---

*God hasn't left us alone to figure out the answers to life's questions all by ourselves. We have a Teacher who is there to help lead and guide us. Ask him what lessons he wants you to learn today.*

# REVEALER OF SECRETS

### Galeh Razin (Aramaic)  גְּלֵה רָזִין

### Daniel 2:29–30, 47

"Your majesty, when you were in bed, you began thinking about what would take place in the future; and he who reveals secrets has revealed to you what will happen. Yet this secret has not been revealed to me because I am wiser than anyone living, but so that the meaning can be made known to your majesty, and then you can understand the thoughts of your own mind."

To Dani'el the king said, "Your God is indeed the God of gods, the Lord of kings and a revealer of secrets, since you have been able to reveal this secret."

### Luke 8:9–10

His *talmidim* [disciples] asked him what this parable might mean, and he said, "To you it has been given to know the secrets of the Kingdom of God; but the rest are taught in parables, so that they may **look but not see, and listen but not understand.**"

### 1 Corinthians 4:4–5

. . . The one who is evaluating me is the Lord. So don't pronounce judgment prematurely, before the Lord comes; for he will bring to light what is now hidden in darkness; he will expose the motives of people's hearts . . .

---

*Are there secrets in your life you hope nobody finds out? There are no secrets with God. He knows and sees all. One day, the motives of our hearts will be revealed. Seek to live a life of humility and honesty before God and with others.*

# JUDGE

*Shofet*     שֹׁפֵט

**Psalm 7:8–9**

May the assembly of the peoples surround you;
may you return to rule over them from on high.
ADONAI, who dispenses judgment to the peoples,
judge me, ADONAI, according to my righteousness
and as my integrity deserves.

**Psalm 50:4, 6**

. . . he calls to the heavens above and to earth,
in order to judge his people.

The heavens proclaim his righteousness,
for God himself is judge.

**Psalm 96:12–13**

. . . let the fields exult and all that is in them.
Then all the trees in the forest will sing
before ADONAI, because he has come,
he has come to judge the earth;
he will judge the world rightly
and the peoples with his faithfulness.

**Acts 10:42–43**

"Then he commanded us to proclaim and attest
to the Jewish people that this man has been
appointed by God to judge the living and the
dead. All the prophets bear witness to him, that
everyone who puts his trust in him receives
forgiveness of sins through his name."

---

*Have you ever heard of a judge that accepted a bribe or was biased in favor of one party? We have a Judge who is upright and honest. All of his rulings are impartial and we can trust him with our lives.*

# THE LORD WHO SETS YOU APART

Adonai M'kadishkhem

**Leviticus 20:8**

"Observe my regulations, and obey them; I am ADONAI, who sets you apart to be holy."

**Exodus 31:13**

"Tell the people of Isra'el, 'You are to observe my *Shabbats* [Sabbaths]; for this is a sign between me and you through all your generations; so that you will know that I am ADONAI, who sets you apart for me."

**John 17:17–19**

"Set them apart for holiness by means of the truth — your word is truth. Just as you sent me into the world. I have sent them into the world. On their behalf I am setting myself apart for holiness, so that they too may be set apart for holiness by means of the truth."

**1 Corinthians 6:11**

Some of you used to do these things. But you have cleansed yourselves, you have been set apart for God, you have come to be counted righteous through the power of the Lord Yeshua the Messiah and the Spirit of our God.

*God gave the people of Isra'el special instructions for holy living, setting them apart for himself, and making them different from the surrounding nations. Are you like all of your neighbors, coworkers, or friends? Ask God to show areas in your life that need to be set apart for him.*

# Morning Star

## Kokhav HaShachar כּוֹכַב הַשַּׁחַר

*2 Peter 1:19*

Yes, we have the prophetic Word made very certain. You will do well to pay attention to it as to a light shining in a dark, murky place, until the Day dawns and the Morning Star rises in your hearts.

*Revelation 2:26–29*

"To him who wins the victory and does what I want until the goal is reached,

**I will give** him authority over the **nations;**
he **will** rule **them with a staff of iron**
**and dash them to pieces like pottery,**

just as I have received authority from my Father. I will also give him the morning star. Those who have ears, let them hear what the Spirit is saying to the Messianic communities."

*Revelation 22:16*

"I, Yeshua, have sent my angel to give you this testimony for the Messianic communities. I am the Root and Offspring of David, the bright Morning Star."

---

*The morning star in the eastern sky at daybreak is a beautiful sight. The dawning of each new day brings another twenty-four hours to love our Morning Star, Yeshua, the one who has risen in our hearts.*

# THE REAL VINE

*Ha Gefen Ha'Amitit*

**John 15:1–5, 7–8**

"I am the real vine, and my Father is the gardener. Every branch which is part of me but fails to bear fruit, he cuts off; and every branch that does bear fruit, he prunes, so that it may bear more fruit. Right now, because of the word which I have spoken to you, you are pruned. Stay united with me, as I will with you — for just as the branch can't put forth fruit by itself apart from the vine, so you can't bear fruit apart from me."

"I am the vine and you are the branches. Those who stay united with me, and I with them, are the ones who bear much fruit; because apart from me you can't do a thing."

"If you remain united with me, and my words with you, then ask whatever you want, and it will happen for you. This is how my Father is glorified — in your bearing much fruit; this is how you will prove to be my *talmidim* [disciples]."

---

*Vines grow along whatever is nearby, latching on with their tendrils. Nourishment flows from the roots to all parts of the plant, causing it to bear fruit in season. Stay close to Yeshua so you can receive spiritual nourishment and bear fruit.*

# GOD OF JUSTICE

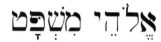 Elohey Mishpat     אֱלֹהֵי מִשְׁפָּט

**Isaiah 30:18**
> Yet ADONAI is just waiting to show you favor,
> he will have pity on you from on high;
> for ADONAI is a God of justice;
> happy are all who wait for him!

**Isaiah 45:23–24**
> "In the name of myself I have sworn,
> from my mouth has rightly gone out,
> a word that will not return —
> that to me every knee will bow
> and every tongue will swear about me
> that only in ADONAI
> are justice and strength. . . ."

**Psalm 97:2**
> Clouds and thick darkness surround him;
> righteousness and justice are the foundation
> of his throne.

**Psalm 99:4**
> "Mighty king who loves justice, you established
> fairness, justice and righteousness in Ya'akov
> [Jacob]."

**Psalm 111:7**
> The works of his hands are truth and justice;
> all his precepts can be trusted.

---

*That's not fair! Have you ever said that? When it seems like you are being taken advantage of, when things don't go your way— be encouraged and wait for God to work. His ways are fair and righteous. Put your trust in him.*

7

*Defender*

*The One Who
Protects Us*

Defender     114

Guardian     115

Ancient One     116

Mighty God     117

The Lord of Victory     118

Lion of Judah     119

God of Zeal     120

Lord of Heaven's Armies     121

My Advocate     122

Shield     123

The Lord My Banner     124

Jealous God     125

God Who Thunders     126

God of Vengeance     127

Stronghold     128

God of Signs and Wonders     129

Warrior     130

# DEFENDER

 *Yariv*     יָרִיב

### Deuteronomy 33:29

Happy are you, Isra'el!
"Who is like you, a people saved by ADONAI,
your defender helping you
and your sword of triumph?
Your enemies will cringe before you,
but you will trample down their high places."

### Isaiah 19:19–20

On that day there will be an altar to ADONAI in the
middle of the land of Egypt, as well as a standing-
stone for ADONAI at its border. It will be a sign and
witness to ADONAI-*Tzva'ot* [Lord of Hosts] in the
land of Egypt; so that when they cry out to
ADONAI for help because of the oppressors, he will
send them a savior to defend and rescue them.

### Psalm 35:23–24

Wake up! Get up, my God, my Lord!
Defend me and my cause!
Give judgment for me, ADONAI, my God,
as your righteousness demands. . . .

### Proverbs 23:10–11

Don't move the ancient boundary stone
   or encroach on the land of the fatherless;
for their Redeemer is strong;
   he will take up their fight against you.

*In the face of predators, animals such as bison and elephants group together, surrounding their young to protect them from danger. We have a Defender who protects us from the attacks of the evil one.*

# GUARDIAN

*Shomer* שׁוֹמֵר

**Genesis 28:15**

"Look, I am with you. I will guard you wherever you go, and I will bring you back into this land, because I won't leave you until I have done what I have promised you."

**Psalm 121:3–8**

He will not let your foot slip —
your guardian is not asleep.
No, the guardian of Isra'el
never slumbers or sleeps.

ADONAI is your guardian; at your right hand
ADONAI provides you with shade —
the sun can't strike you during the day
or even the moon at night.

ADONAI will guard you against all harm;
he will guard your life.
ADONAI will guard your coming and going
from now on and forever.

**Psalm 127:1**

. . . Unless ADONAI guards the city,
the guard keeps watch in vain.

**1 John 5:18**

We know that everyone who has God as his Father does not go on sinning; on the contrary, the Son born of God protects him, and the Evil One does not touch him.

---

*In Israel, all soldiers must do guard duty. The constant attentiveness, long hours, and desert heat can be wearying. Let us be thankful for a Guardian who never gets weary of keeping watch over us.*

# ANCIENT ONE

*Atik Yomaiya (Aramaic)*

**Daniel 7:9–10, 13–14, 21–22**

"As I watched, thrones were set in place;
and the Ancient One took his seat.
His clothing was as white as snow,
the hair of his head was white like wool.
His throne was fiery flames,
with wheels of burning fire.
A stream of fire flowed from his presence;
thousands and thousands ministered to him,
millions and millions stood before him. . . ."

"I kept watching the night visions,
when I saw, coming with the clouds of heaven,
someone like a son of man.

He approached the Ancient One
and was led into his presence.
To him was given rulership,
glory and a kingdom,
so that all peoples, nations and languages
should serve him.
His rulership is an eternal rulership
that will not pass away . . ."

"I watched, and that horn made war with the
holy ones and was winning, until the Ancient
One came, judgment was given in favor of the
holy ones of the Most High, and the time came
for the holy ones to take over the kingdom."

---

*Look up the definition of "ancient" and you'll see words like "old," "archaic," "antiquated," and "obsolete." However, God is none of these things. Through this name, we understand a little more about God's immortality, wisdom, and power. Praise him!*

# MIGHTY GOD

*El Gibbor*     אֵל גִּבּוֹר

**Joshua 22:22**

"The Mighty One, God, is ADONAI!"

**Isaiah 9:5**

For a child is born to us,
a son is given to us;
dominion will rest on his shoulders,
and he will be given the name
Pele-Yo'etz El Gibbor
Avi-'Ad Sar-Shalom
[Wonder of a Counselor, Mighty God,
Father of Eternity, Prince of Peace].

**Isaiah 10:21**

A remnant will return,
the remnant of Ya'akov [Jacob],
to the mighty God.

**Psalm 24:7–8**

Lift up your heads, you gates!
Lift them up, everlasting doors,
so that the glorious king can enter!
Who is he, this glorious king?
ADONAI, strong and mighty,
ADONAI, mighty in battle.

**Psalm 50:1**

. . . The Mighty One, God, ADONAI, is speaking,
summoning the world from east to west. . . .

*Mighty! Imposing, awesome, and omnipotent. Who can compare to our God? He is mightier and more powerful than any army. He commands and it is so.*

# THE LORD OF VICTORY

*Adonai Hoshia*　　　　יְהוָה הוֹשִׁיעַ

**Deuteronomy 20:3–4**

". . . You are about to do battle against your enemies. Don't be fainthearted or afraid; don't be alarmed or frightened by them; because ADONAI your God is going with you to fight on your behalf against your enemies and give you victory."

**Zechariah 9:9**

"Rejoice with all your heart, daughter of Tziyon [Zion]! Shout out loud, daughter of Yerushalayim!*
Look! Your king is coming to you.
He is righteous, and he is victorious.
Yet he is humble — he's riding on a donkey, yes, on a lowly donkey's colt."

**Psalm 20:7, 10**

Now I know that ADONAI
gives victory to his anointed one —
he will answer him from his holy heaven
with mighty victories by his right hand.

Give victory, ADONAI!
Let the King answer us the day we call.

**1 Corinthians 15:56–57**

The sting of death is sin; and sin draws its power from the *Torah* [teaching]; but thanks be to God, who gives us the victory through our Lord Yeshua the Messiah!

*Jerusalem

*Are you losing battles left and right? Do you sometimes feel like no matter what you do, you can't win? Do you feel like a failure? Look to the Lord of Victory. He longs to help you become victorious!*

# LION OF JUDAH

*Aryeh Mishevet Y'hudah*          אַרְיֵה מִשֵּׁבֶט יְהוּדָה

### Hosea 5:14; 6:1

"For to Efrayim [Ephraim] I will be like a lion,
and like a young lion to the house of Y'hudah
[Judah] — I will tear them up and go away;
I will carry them off, and no one will rescue."

"Come, let us return to ADONAI:
for he has torn, and he will heal us;
he has struck, and he will bind our wounds."

### Revelation 5:4–5, 9

I cried and cried, because no one was found
worthy to open the scroll or look inside it. One
of the elders said to me, "Don't cry. Look, the
Lion of the tribe of Y'hudah, the Root of
David, has won the right to open the scroll and
its seven seals."

". . . You are worthy to take the scroll and
break its seals;
because you were slaughtered;
at the cost of blood you ransomed for God
persons from every tribe, language, people
and nation."

---

*The image of a lion has long been a Jewish symbol. It was used for King Solomon's throne and is used today in ritual objects. These beautiful yet fierce animals represent power and strength. The mighty Lion of the tribe of Y'hudah allowed himself to be slaughtered as a gentle Lamb so we could be worthy to stand in his presence.*

# GOD OF ZEAL

El Kin'ah     אֵל קַנָּאה

*2 Kings 19:30–31*
"Meanwhile, the remnant
of the house of Y'hudah [Judah] that has escaped
will again take root downward
and bear fruit upward;
for a remnant will go out from Yerushalayim
[Jerusalem], those escaping will go out from
Mount Tziyon [Zion].
The zeal of ADONAI-*Tzva'ot* [Lord of Hosts]
will accomplish this."

*Isaiah 9:6*
. . . in order to extend the dominion
and perpetuate the peace
of the throne and kingdom of David,
to secure it and sustain it
through justice and righteousness
henceforth and forever.
The zeal of ADONAI-*Tzva'ot*
will accomplish this.

*Isaiah 59:16–17*
He saw that there was no one,
was amazed that no one interceded.
Therefore his own arm brought him salvation,
and his own righteousness sustained him.
He put on righteousness as his breastplate,
salvation as a helmet on his head;
he clothed himself with garments of vengeance
and wrapped himself in a mantle of zeal.

*What kinds of things are you zealous for? What drives you day-by-day? God's intense, devoted drive to accomplish his purposes is without equal. He is passionate and tireless as he carries out his plans. Imitate God and be zealous for the things that please him.*

# LORD OF HEAVEN'S ARMIES (LORD OF HOSTS)

## *Adonai Tzva'ot*

יהוה צְבָאוֹת

### Joshua 5:13–15

One day . . . Y'hoshua [Joshua] . . . raised his eyes and looked; and in front of him stood a man with his drawn sword in his hand. Y'hoshua went over to him and asked him, "Are you on our side or on the side of our enemies?" "No," he replied, "but I am the commander of ADONAI's army; I have come just now." Y'hoshua fell down with his face to the ground and worshiped him, then asked, "What does my lord have to say to his servant?" The commander of ADONAI's army answered Y'hoshua, "Take your sandals off your feet, because the place where you are standing is holy." And Y'hoshua did so.

### Psalm 84:4

As the sparrow finds herself a home and the swallow her nest, where she lays her young, [so my resting-place is] by your altars, ADONAI-*Tzva'ot*, my king and my God.

### Revelation 11:16–17

The twenty-four elders sitting on their thrones in God's presence fell on their faces and worshiped God, saying,

"We thank you, ADONAI, **God of heaven's armies,** the One who is and was . . ."

---

*The Commander of the hosts of heaven is mighty and powerful. He is worthy of our worship and highest praise. And though he is awe inspiring, terrifying, and holy, we can approach him and say as the psalmist did, "my resting place is by your altars, ADONAI Tzva'ot, my king and my God."*

# My Advocate

 *Sahadi* שָׂהֲדִי

**Psalm 119:153–154**

Look at my distress, and rescue me,
for I do not forget your *Torah* [teaching].
Plead my cause, and redeem me;
in keeping with your promise, revive me.

**Proverbs 22:22–23**

Don't exploit the helpless, because they are
helpless, and don't crush the poor in court,
for ADONAI will plead their case for them
and withhold life from those who defraud them.

**Job 16:19**

Even now, my witness is in heaven;
my advocate is there on high.

**1 John 2:1**

My children, I am writing you these things so that
you won't sin. But if anyone does sin, we have
Yeshua the Messiah, the *Tzaddik* [Righteous One],
who pleads our cause with the Father.

---

*Have you ever needed a lawyer to plead your case? An advocate believes in you, stands with you and for you, and defends you when you are accused. Be grateful for Yeshua the Messiah, your advocate. Through him, the verdict is "not guilty." You won't find a more competent attorney!*

# SHIELD

Magen    מָגֵן

**Psalm 3:4**
But you, ADONAI, are a shield for me;
you are my glory, you lift my head high.

**Psalm 7:11**
My shield is God,
who saves the upright in heart.

**Psalm 18:36**
"You give me your shield, which is salvation,
your right hand holds me up,
your humility makes me great."

**Psalm 28:7**
ADONAI is my strength and shield;
in him my heart trusted, and I have been
helped. . . .

**Psalm 33:20**
We are waiting for ADONAI;
he is our help and shield.

**Proverbs 2:7**
He stores up common sense for the upright,
is a shield to those whose conduct is blameless.

*Imagine fierce warriors, standing shield-to-shield, impenetrable, wielding their spears. This is a picture of the way God protects those who are upright in heart. He stops the arrows and darts of the enemy. Nothing gets past him!*

# THE LORD MY BANNER

## Adonai Nissi יהוה נִסִּי

**Exodus 17:14–16**

ADONAI said to Moshe [Moses], "Write this in a book to be remembered, and tell it to Y'hoshua [Joshua]: I will completely blot out any memory of 'Amalek from under heaven." Moshe built an altar, called it ADONAI *Nissi*, and said, "Because their hand was against the throne of *Yah*,* ADONAI will fight 'Amalek generation after generation."

**Isaiah 11:12**

He will hoist a banner for the *Goyim* [nations], assemble the dispersed of Isra'el, and gather the scattered of Y'hudah [Judah] from the four corners of the earth.

*a name of God

**Isaiah 49:22**

Adonai ELOHIM [Lord God] answers:
"I am beckoning to the nations, raising my banner for the peoples.
They will bring your sons in their arms and carry your daughters on their shoulders."

**Song of Solomon 2:4**

He brings me to the banquet hall; his banner over me is love.

*Each nation has a flag or banner that represents who they are. God's banner of love is over us declaring to all who see, that the Lord is our God, and we are his people.*

# JEALOUS GOD

*El Kana*     אֵל קַנָּא

**Deuteronomy 6:13–15**

"You are to fear *ADONAI* your God, serve him and swear by his name. You are not to follow other gods, chosen from the gods of the peoples around you; because *ADONAI*, your God, who is here with you, is a jealous God . . ."

**Exodus 34:14**

". . . because you are not to bow down to any other god; since *ADONAI* — whose very name is Jealous — is a jealous God."

**Ezekiel 39:25**

"Therefore *Adonai* ELOHIM [Lord God] says this: 'Now I will restore the fortunes of Ya'akov [Jacob] and have compassion on the entire house of Isra'el, and I will be jealous for my holy name.'"

**Zechariah 8:2**

"*ADONAI-Tzva'ot* [Lord of Hosts] says, 'I am extremely jealous on Tziyon's [Zion's] behalf, and I am jealous for her with great fury.'"

---

*Because God loves us, he is jealous for our love. We cannot seek his face when we put our own interests ahead of his. He will not accept anything less than our whole heart. Have you given God first place in your life?*

# GOD WHO THUNDERS

 *El Hir'im* אֵל הִרְעִים

**Jeremiah 51:15–16**
> He made the earth by his power,
> established the world by his wisdom
> spread out the sky by his understanding.
> When he thunders, the waters in heaven roar,
> he raises clouds from the ends of the earth,
> he makes the lightning flash in the rain
> and brings the wind out from his storehouses.

**Joel 4:16**
> ADONAI will roar from Tziyon [Zion],
> he will thunder from Yerushalayim [Jerusalem],
> the sky and the earth will shake.

**Psalm 29:3**
> The voice of ADONAI is over the waters;
> the God of glory thunders . . .

**Job 37:5**
> "God thunders wonderfully with his voice,
> he does great things beyond our understanding."

---

*Have you ever been afraid of thunder and lightning? When thunder rolls and cracks of lightning split the night sky, the ground can shake and startle us. The next time you hear rolling thunder, turn to God and listen carefully. He might be trying to tell you something.*

# GOD OF VENGEANCE

*El N'kamot*     אֵל נְקָמוֹת

**Ezekiel 25:16–17**

"*Adonai* ELOHIM [Lord God] says, 'I will stretch out my hand over the P'lishtim [Philistines], eliminate the K'reti [Kerethites] and destroy the rest of the seacoast peoples. I will execute great vengeance on them with furious punishments; and they will know that I am ADONAI when I lay my vengeance on them.'"

**Nahum 1:2**

ADONAI is a jealous and vengeful God.
ADONAI avenges; he knows how to be angry.
ADONAI takes vengeance on his foes
and stores up wrath for his enemies.

**Psalm 94:1–2**

God of vengeance, ADONAI!
God of vengeance, appear!
Assert yourself as judge of the earth!
Pay back the proud as they deserve!

**Romans 12:19**

Never seek revenge, my friends; instead, leave that to God's anger; for in the *Tanakh* it is written,

"ADONAI says, 'Vengeance is my responsibility; I will repay.'"

---

*It's tempting to want to get even when we are wronged, to hurt others as they hurt us. But God has a better way. The next time you feel like "getting back" at someone, remember what God said, "Vengeance is my responsibility."*

# STRONGHOLD

*Ma'oz* מָעוֹז

**Nahum 1:7**
ADONAI is good,
a stronghold in time of trouble;
he takes care of those
who take refuge in him.

**Joel 4:16**
. . . But ADONAI will be a refuge for his people,
a stronghold for the people of Isra'el.

**Psalm 9:10**
ADONAI is a stronghold for the oppressed,
a tower of strength in times of trouble.

**Psalm 27:1**
ADONAI is my light and salvation;
whom do I need to fear?
ADONAI is the stronghold of my life;
of whom should I be afraid?

**Psalm 37:39–40**
ADONAI is the one who saves the righteous;
he is their stronghold in time of trouble.
ADONAI helps them and rescues them,
rescues them from the wicked and saves them;
because they take refuge in him.

---

*Forts and walls built by men can be breached. But we have a stronghold that can never be moved or destroyed. The next time you need a secure place to go when difficulties abound, do not fear. God is your tower of strength in times of trouble.*

# GOD OF SIGNS AND WONDERS

*El Otot V'moftim*

אֵל אֹתֹת וּמוֹפְתִים

### Exodus 7:3
"But I will make him hardhearted. Even though I will increase my signs and wonders in the land of Egypt."

### Deuteronomy 26:8–9
". . . and ADONAI brought us out of Egypt with a strong hand and a stretched-out arm, with great terror, and with signs and wonders. Now he has brought us to this place and given us this land, a land flowing with milk and honey."

### Daniel 3:33
"How great are his signs!
How powerful his wonders!
His kingdom lasts forever,
and he rules all generations."

### Acts 4:30, 15:12
"Stretch out your hand to heal and to do signs and miracles through the name of your holy servant Yeshua!"

Then the whole assembly kept still as they listened to Bar-Nabba [Barnabas] and Sha'ul [Paul] tell what signs and miracles God had done through them among the Gentiles.

---

*When something miraculous happens, contradicting "scientific" laws, such as the recovery of someone close to death, it's often referred to as an "act of God." Catastrophic events are often called "acts of God" as well. God can do anything to get our attention and declare his power. Is he trying to show you something today?*

# WARRIOR

Ish Milchamah

**Exodus 15:3**
"ADONAI is a warrior;
ADONAI is his name."

**Isaiah 42:13**
ADONAI will go out like a soldier,
like a soldier roused to the fury of battle;
he will shout, yes, he raises the battle cry;
as he triumphs over his foes.

**Jeremiah 20:11**
But ADONAI is with me like a dreaded warrior;
so my persecutors will stumble, defeated,
greatly ashamed because of their failure . . .

**Psalm 78:65–66**
Then *Adonai* awoke, as if from sleep,
like a warrior shouting for joy from wine.
He struck his foes, driving them back
and putting them to perpetual shame.

---

*Our God is a triumphant Champion greater than any battle hero. He vanquishes his foes and strikes down all his enemies. And he wages war on our behalf. Put your trust in God and let him fight your battles for you.*

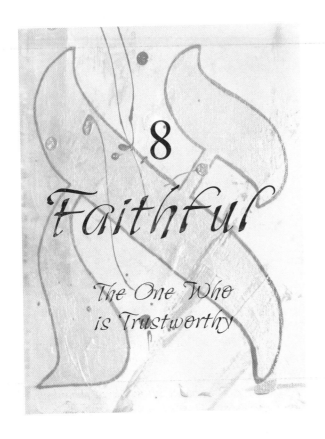

8

# Faithful

## The One Who is Trustworthy

Faithful God    132

Lord God of the Hebrews    133

My Portion    134

The Rock    135

Bridegroom    136

True and Faithful Witness    137

Restorer    138

Friend    139

God of Our Fathers    140

My Chosen One    141

Very Great Reward    142

My Hope    143

God Who Remembers    144

Husband    145

My Beloved    146

The Prophet    147

The First and the Last    148

# FAITHFUL GOD

 *El Ne'eman*     אֵל נֶאֱמָן

**Deuteronomy 7:8–9**
"Rather, it was because ADONAI loved you, and because he wanted to keep the oath which he had sworn to your ancestors, that ADONAI brought you out with a strong hand and redeemed you from a life of slavery under the hand of Pharaoh king of Egypt. From this you can know that ADONAI your God is indeed God, the faithful God, who keeps his covenant and extends grace to those who love him and observe his *mitzvot* [commandments], to a thousand generations."

**2 Chronicles 1:9–10**
"Now, ADONAI, God, you have been faithful to your promise to David my father; for you have made me king over a people as numerous as the grains of dust on the earth. So now, give me wisdom and knowledge; so that I will be able to lead this people. . . ."

**1 Thessalonians 5:24**
The one calling you is faithful, and he will do it.

---

*Loyal and unwavering, steadfast and reliable, constant and dependable, upright and trustworthy, always keeps a promise. These are qualities of a faithful person—and of God. He accomplishes everything he says he will do. Put your hope and trust in him. He will never let you down.*

# LORD GOD OF THE HEBREWS

*Adonai Elohey Ha'Ivriyim*

יהוה אֱלֹהֵי הָעִבְרִיִּים

### Exodus 3:18, 7:15–16, 9:1, 10:3

"They will heed what you say. Then you will come, you and the leaders of Isra'el, before the king of Egypt; and you will tell him, 'ADONAI, the God of the Hebrews, has met with us. Now, please, let us go three days' journey into the desert; so that we can sacrifice to ADONAI our God.'"

"Go to Pharaoh in the morning when he goes out to the water. Stand on the riverbank to confront him, take in your hand the staff which was turned into a snake, and say to him, 'ADONAI, the God of the Hebrews, sent me to you to say: "Let my people go, so that they can worship me in the desert." But until now you haven't listened.'"

Then ADONAI said to Moshe [Moses], "Go to Pharaoh, and tell him, 'Here is what ADONAI, the God of the Hebrews, says: "Let my people go, so that they can worship me."'"

Moshe and Aharon [Aaron] went in to Pharaoh and said to him, "Here is what ADONAI, God of the Hebrews, says: 'How much longer will you refuse to submit to me? Let my people go, so that they can worship me.'"

---

*The Egyptians learned the hard way. The God of the Hebrews was the one true God—greater than Pharaoh, and more powerful than any of their man-made gods. The God of the Hebrews is still delivering his people. Are there any false gods in your life that are keeping you from worshiping him freely?*

# MY PORTION

 Helki חֶלְקִי

**Jeremiah 10:16**
Ya'akov's [Jacob's] portion is not like these,
for he is the one who formed all things.
Isra'el is the tribe he claims as his heritage;
ADONAI-Tzva'ot [Lord of Hosts] is his name.

**Psalm 16:5–6**
ADONAI, my assigned portion, my cup:
you safeguard my share.
Pleasant places were measured out for me;
I am content with my heritage.

**Psalm 73:26**
My mind and my body may fail; but God
is the rock for my mind and my portion forever.

**Psalm 142:6**
I cried out to you, ADONAI;
I said, "You are my refuge,
my portion in the land of the living."

*Have you ever felt like you didn't get what you deserved? Do you struggle finding contentment? Is it tempting to compare your life to the lives of others? Be encouraged. God is abundantly more than enough. He knows the "portion" you've received and what you need even before you ask. He is all you need.*

# THE ROCK

*HaTzur*     הַצּוּר

**Deuteronomy 32:3–4**

"For I will proclaim the name of ADONAI.
Come, declare the greatness of our God!
The Rock! His work is perfect,
for all his ways are just. . . ."

**Isaiah 26:3–4**

"A person whose desire rests on you
you preserve in perfect peace,
because he trusts in you.
Trust in ADONAI forever,
because in *Yah*\* ADONAI
is a Rock of Ages."

**Psalm 144:1**

Blessed be ADONAI, my rock,
who trains my hands for war
and my fingers for battle.

**1 Corinthians 10:3–4**

. . . also they all ate the same food from the
Spirit, and they all drank the same drink from
the Spirit — for they drank from a Spirit-sent
Rock which followed them, and that Rock was
the Messiah.

\*a name of God

*The expression, "like the rock of Gibraltar" has come to mean something or someone that is impressive, dependable, steady, and immovable. God is our rock-solid place. Firmly plant your feet on The Rock and you will not be moved, no matter what storms of life come crashing your way.*

# BRIDEGROOM

*Hatan*    חָתָן

**Isaiah 62:4–5**

You will no longer be spoken of as 'Azuvah
[Abandoned] or your land be spoken of as
'Sh'mamah [Desolate];
rather, you will be called Heftzi-Vah
[My-Delight-Is-In-Her]
and your land Be'ulah [Married].
For ADONAI delights in you,
and your land will be married —
as a young man marries a young woman,
your sons will marry you;
as a bridegroom rejoices over the bride,
your God will rejoice over you.

**Matthew 9:14–15**

Next, Yochanan's [John's] *talmidim* [disciples]
came to him and asked, "Why is it that we and
the *P'rushim* [Pharisees] fast frequently, but your
*talmidim* don't fast at all?" Yeshua said to them,
"Can wedding guests mourn while the
bridegroom is still with them? But the time will
come when the bridegroom is taken away from
them; then they will fast."

*In a Jewish wedding ceremony, the bridegroom places a gold ring on the finger of his beloved and recites,
"Behold, you are sanctified [set apart] to me with this ring, according to the Law of Moses and of Israel."
Yeshua is our Bridegroom. He rejoices over us, loves us, and has set us apart for himself.*

# TRUE AND FAITHFUL WITNESS

*'Ed Emet V'ne'eman*

**Jeremiah 42:5**

They said to Yirmeyahu [Jeremiah], "May ADONAI be a true and faithful witness against us if we fail to do any part of what ADONAI your God gives you to tell us."

**John 8:18**

"I myself testify on my own behalf, and so does the Father who sent me."

**Romans 8:16**

The Spirit himself bears witness with our own spirits that we are children of God.

**Revelation 1:4–5**

. . . Grace and *shalom* [peace] to you from the One who is, who was and who is coming; from the sevenfold Spirit before his throne; and from Yeshua the Messiah, the faithful witness, the firstborn from the dead and the ruler of the earth's kings. . . .

**Revelation 3:14**

"To the angel of the Messianic Community in Laodicea, write: 'Here is the message from the *Amen*, the faithful and true witness, the Ruler of God's creation.'"

---

*A witness testifies to what they have seen, heard, or experienced. Their personal knowledge of facts helps to acquit the innocent or indict the guilty. God, you know our thoughts and everything we have done. We're not blameless. Thank you for the testimony of Yeshua. Through faith in him, we are pronounced innocent.*

# RESTORER

M'shivah  מְשִׁיבָה

**Isaiah 38:16**
"*Adonai*, by these things people live;
in all these is the life of my spirit.
You're restoring my health and giving me life."

**Isaiah 62:6–7**
I have posted watchmen
on your walls, Yerushalayim [Jerusalem];
they will never fall silent,
neither by day nor by night.
You who call on ADONAI,
give yourselves no rest;
and give him no rest till he restores Yerushalayim
and makes it a praise on earth.

**Psalm 19:8**
The *Torah* [teaching] of ADONAI is perfect,
restoring the inner person. . . .

**Acts 3:21**
He has to remain in heaven until the time comes
for restoring everything, as God said long ago,
when he spoke through the holy prophets.

**1 Peter 5:10**
You will have to suffer only a little while; after
that, God, who is full of grace, the one who
called you to his eternal glory in union with the
Messiah, will himself restore, establish and
strengthen you and make you firm.

---

*Have you ever restored a piece of old furniture, stripping away the layers of paint and varnish that hid the beauty of the original wood? God is in the restoration business. Talk to him about the things in your life that need restoring. Let him bring out your hidden beauty and restore the worn places in your life.*

# FRIEND

 Ohev    אֹהֵב

### Exodus 33:11
ADONAI would speak to Moshe [Moses] face to face, as a man speaks to his friend. . . .

### 2 Chronicles 20:7
"You, our God, drove out those living in the land ahead of your people Isra'el and gave it forever to the descendants of Avraham [Abraham] your friend."

### Luke 5:20
When Yeshua saw their trust, he said, "Friend, your sins are forgiven you."

### James 2:23
. . . and the passage of the *Tanakh* was fulfilled which says, **"Avraham had faith in God, and it was credited to his account as righteousness."** He was even called **God's friend.**

---

*Faithful friends are hard to find. But we have a Friend who will never reject us, move away, or desert us in times of trouble. We have a Friend who is loyal and true, always available, and there when we need to talk, a friend who sticks right by us. Thank you God, for being my friend.*

# GOD OF OUR FATHERS

*Elohey Avoteynu*　אֱלֹהֵי אֲבֹתֵינוּ

### Exodus 3:6

"I am the God of your father," he continued, "the God of Avraham [Abraham], the God of Yitz'chak [Isaac] and the God of Ya'akov [Jacob]." Moshe [Moses] covered his face, because he was afraid to look at God.

### Deuteronomy 26:7–8

"So we cried out to ADONAI, the God of our ancestors. ADONAI heard us and saw our misery, toil and oppression; and ADONAI brought us out of Egypt with a strong hand and a stretched-out arm, with great terror, and with signs and wonders."

### 1 Chronicles 29:18

"ADONAI, God of Avraham, Yitz'chak and Isra'el our ancestors, guard forever the inclinations of the thoughts in the hearts of your people; direct their hearts to you."

### Acts 5:30

**The God of our fathers** raised up Yeshua . . .

### Acts 22:14

"He said, 'The **God of our fathers** determined in advance that you should know his will, see the *Tzaddik* [Righteous One] and hear his voice.'"

---

*The God that Abraham, Isaac, and Jacob called their own is still our God today. He revealed himself to them and their descendents. He delivered the children of Israel from slavery and has always been faithful to work mightily on behalf of all those who call on him. Call on him today.*

# MY CHOSEN ONE

B'chiri     בְּחִירִי

### Isaiah 42:1

"Here is my servant, whom I support,
my chosen one, in whom I take pleasure.
I have put my Spirit on him;
he will bring justice to the *Goyim* [nations]."

### Luke 23:35

The people stood **watching**, and the rulers
**sneered** at him. "He saved others," they said,
"so if he really is the Messiah, the one chosen
by God, let him save himself!"

### 1 Peter 2:4–6

As you come to him, the living **stone**, rejected by
people but **chosen** by God and **precious** to him,
you yourselves, as living **stones**, are being built
into a spiritual house to be *cohanim* [priests] set
apart for God to offer spiritual sacrifices
acceptable to him through Yeshua the Messiah.
This is why the *Tanakh* says,

> "Look! I am laying in Tziyon [Zion] a stone,
> a chosen and precious cornerstone;
> and whoever rests his trust on it
> will certainly not be humiliated."

---

*Chosen—called, selected, favored, and set apart for a special purpose. Throughout the Scriptures, we read about individuals who were chosen to serve God and declare his glory. Often, their paths were difficult and filled with suffering. God, thank you for Yeshua, the One chosen to suffer. Through him, we see your glory.*

# Very Great Reward

S'khar Harbeh M'od     שָׂכָר הַרְבֵּה מְאֹד

**Genesis 15:1**
Some time later the word of ADONAI came to Avram [Abram] in a vision: "Don't be afraid, Avram. I am your protector; your reward will be very great."

**1 Samuel 26:23**
"ADONAI will give every person a reward suited to his uprightness and faithfulness. . . ."

**Isaiah 40:10**
"Here comes *Adonai* ELOHIM [Lord God] with power, and his arm will rule for him.
Look! His reward is with him,
and his recompense is before him."

**Matthew 5:12**
"Rejoice, be glad, because your reward in heaven is great . . ."

**Hebrews 10:35–36**
So don't throw away that courage of yours, which carries with it such a great reward. For you need to hold out; so that, by having done what God wills, you may receive what he has promised.

---

*Rewards are given for acts of service, for helping to find a criminal or a lost puppy. The prefix "re" indicates that by their very nature, they are a return or recompense for something we have done. The rewards of this life pale in comparison to what God will give to those who follow him faithfully.*

# MY HOPE

*Tikvati* תִּקְוָתִי

### Psalm 52:11
I will praise you forever for what you have done,
and I will put my hope in your name;
for this is what is good
in the presence of your faithful.

### Psalm 71:5
For you are my hope, *Adonai* ELOHIM [Lord God],
in whom I have trusted since I was young.

### Romans 15:13
May God, the source of hope, fill you completely
with joy and *shalom* [peace] as you continue trusting, so that by the power of the *Ruach HaKodesh*
[Holy Spirit] you may overflow with hope.

### Hebrews 6:18–19
. . . so that through two unchangeable things, in
neither of which God could lie, we, who have
fled to take a firm hold on the hope set before
us, would be strongly encouraged. We have this
hope as a sure and safe anchor for ourselves . . .

### 1 Peter 1:3–4
Praised be God, Father of our Lord Yeshua the
Messiah, who, in keeping with his great mercy,
has caused us, through the resurrection of Yeshua
the Messiah from the dead, to be born again to a
living hope, to an inheritance that cannot decay,
spoil or fade, kept safe for you in heaven.

---

*Have you ever been disappointed? Have you ever lost heart, hoping for something that did not come
about? To hope means to look forward to something, or trust in someone with confidence and expectation.
We have a God that will never disappoint us when we put our hope in him.*

# GOD WHO REMEMBERS

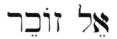 *El Zokher*     אֵל זוֹכֵר

### Genesis 8:1
God remembered Noach [Noah], every living thing and all the livestock with him in the ark; so God caused a wind to pass over the earth, and the water began to go down.

### Genesis 19:29
But when God destroyed the cities of the plain, he remembered Avraham [Abraham] and sent Lot out, away from the destruction, when he overthrew the cities in which Lot lived.

### Exodus 2:23–25
Sometime during those many years the king of Egypt died, but the people of Isra'el still groaned under the yoke of slavery, and they cried out, and their cry for rescue from slavery came up to God. God heard their groaning, and God remembered his covenant with Avraham, Yitz'chak [Isaac] and Ya'akov [Jacob]. God saw the people of Isra'el, and God acknowledged them.

### Isaiah 49:14–16
"But Tziyon [Zion] says, 'ADONAI has abandoned me, *Adonai* has forgotten me.'
Can a woman forget her child at the breast, not show pity on the child from her womb?
Even if these were to forget, I would not forget you.
I have engraved you on the palms of my hands . . ."

---

*Have you ever felt that God has forgotten you? Have you been waiting a long time to see the fulfillment of a promise he made? Trust in God. He is absolutely incapable of forgetting about you. You are engraved on the palms of his hands.*

# HUSBAND

Ba'al  בַּעַל

### Isaiah 54:5

For your husband is your Maker,
ADONAI-Tzva'ot [Lord of Hosts] is his name. . . .

### Jeremiah 31:30–31

"Here, the days are coming," says ADONAI, "when I will make a new covenant with the house of Isra'el and with the house of Y'hudah [Judah]. It will not be like the covenant I made with their fathers on the day I took them by their hand and brought them out of the land of Egypt; because they, for their part, violated my covenant, even though I, for my part, was a husband to them," says ADONAI.

### 2 Corinthians 11:2

For I am jealous for you with God's kind of jealousy; since I promised to present you as a pure virgin in marriage to your one husband, the Messiah.

---

*The heartbreak of a shattered marriage, an unfaithful spouse, or a lost love—many have experienced such pain. But we have a Husband who always cares for, provides for, and protects us. He will never leave. He will always remain faithful to his marriage covenant with us.*

# My Beloved

*Y'didi*  יְדִידִי

**Matthew 3:13, 16–17**

Then Yeshua came from the Galil [Galilee] to the Yarden [Jordan] to be immersed by Yochanan [John]. . . . As soon as Yeshua had been immersed, he came up out of the water. At that moment heaven was opened, he saw the Spirit of God coming down upon him like a dove, and a voice from heaven said, "This is my Son, whom I love; I am well pleased with him."

**Matthew 12:18**

"Here is my servant, whom I have chosen,
my beloved, with whom I am well pleased;
I will put my Spirit on him,
and he will announce justice to the Gentiles."

**Mark 9:2, 7–8**

Six days later, Yeshua took Kefa [Peter], Ya'akov [James] and Yochanan and led them up a high mountain privately. As they watched, he began to change form . . . Then a cloud enveloped them; and a voice came out of the cloud, "This is my Son, whom I love. Listen to him!" Suddenly, when they looked around, they no longer saw anyone with them except Yeshua.

**Ephesians 1:5–6**

He determined in advance that through Yeshua the Messiah we would be his sons — in keeping with his pleasure and purpose — so that we would bring him praise commensurate with the glory of the grace he gave us through the Beloved One.

---

*Can you call Yeshua your Beloved? Does saying that come easily to you or make you uncomfortable? Have you experienced God's love? If not, ask him to reveal himself to you today. He longs for you to know his love.*

# THE PROPHET

*HaNavi*　　הַנָּבִיא

### Deuteronomy 18:15–19

"ADONAI will raise up for you a prophet like me from among yourselves, from your own kinsmen. You are to pay attention to him, just as when you were assembled at Horev [Horeb] and requested ADONAI your God, 'Don't let me hear the voice of ADONAI my God any more, or let me see this great fire ever again; if I do, I will die!' On that occasion ADONAI said to me, 'They are right in what they are saying. I will raise up for them a prophet like you from among their kinsmen. I will put my words in his mouth, and he will tell them everything I order him.

Whoever doesn't listen to my words, which he will speak in my name, will have to account for himself to me.'"

### John 6:14

When the people saw the miracle he had performed, they said, "This has to be 'the prophet' who is supposed to come into the world."

### John 7:40–41

On hearing his words, some people in the crowd said, "Surely this man is 'the prophet'"; others said, "This is the Messiah." . . .

---

*Mediums, astrologers, and card-readers. Some people will pay anything for false information about their future. But God's standard for prophetic accuracy is 100%. Listen to Yeshua, The Prophet. All of his words are true. God holds your future in his hands.*

# THE FIRST AND THE LAST

HaRishon V'Ha'Acharon

### Isaiah 41:4

Whose work is this? Who has brought it about?
He who called the generations from the beginning,
"I, ADONAI, am the first;
and I am the same with those who are last."

### Isaiah 48:12–13

"Listen to me, Ya'akov [ Jacob];
Isra'el, whom I have called;
I am he who is first; I am also the last.
My hand laid the foundation of the earth,
my right hand spread out the heavens
when I summoned them,
at once they rose into being."

### Revelation 1:17–18

When I saw him, I fell down at his feet like a
dead man. He placed his right hand upon me and
said, "Don't be afraid! I am the First and the
Last, the Living One. I was dead, but look! —
I am alive forever and ever! . . ."

### Revelation 22:12–13

"Pay attention!" [says Yeshua,] "I am coming
soon, and my rewards are with me to give to
each person according to what he has done. I am
the 'A' and the 'Z,' the First and the Last, the
Beginning and the End."

---

*There was never a time when God didn't exist. He is the beginning and the end. He is first because he always was, he is last because he will always be, and he is everything in between. He is wonderful and his names are wonderful so worship and praise him with all of your heart!*

# INDEX OF NAMES

Ancient One    116

Anointed One (Messiah)    42

Breath of Life    82

Bridegroom    136

Close God, The    23

Comforter    84

Consuming Fire    94

Cornerstone    61

Covering    79

Creator    28

Defender    114

Dwelling Place    88

Enthroned One    16

Everlasting God    26

Face of God—Presence    89

Faithful God    132

Father    22

Father of Eternity    32

First and the Last, The    148

Forgiving God    25

Friend    139

Gate, The    67

Giver of the Torah    33

God Almighty    2

God in Heaven    13

God is With Us    55

God Most High    12

God of All Encouragement    74

God of Compassion    29

God of Glory    10

God of Israel    37

God of Justice    112

God of Kindness    30

God of Love    31

God of My Life    72

God of My Praise    93

God of My Salvation    41

God of Our Fathers    140

God of Signs and Wonders    129

God of Vengeance    127

God of Zeal    120

God Who Carries You    76

God Who Formed Us
in the Womb    27

God Who Remembers    144

God Who Sees    35

God Who Sustains Me    73

God Who Thunders    126

God, My God    24

God's Lamb    46

God's Only Son    50

Great God    20

Great High Priest    51

Greatness on High, The    8

Guardian    115

Guide    62

Head Over All    7

Hiding Place    64

High, Exalted One    3

Him Who Knows Everything    97

Holy One of Israel    6

Holy Spirit    78

Husband    145

I Am That I Am    4

Jealous God    125

Judge    108

King of Kings    9

King of the Nations    18

Light of Israel    99

Light of the World    101
Lion of Judah    119
Living Bread    102
Living God    5
Living Water    83
Lord God of the Hebrews    133
Lord is Good, The    65
Lord is One, The    17
Lord is There, The    71
Lord My Banner, The    124
Lord My Strength, The    75
Lord of All the Earth    11
Lord of Heaven's Armies
    (Lord of Hosts)    121
Lord of Lords    14
Lord of the Sabbath    52
Lord of Victory, The    118
Lord Our Father, The    38
Lord Our Maker, The    36
Lord Who Has Anointed
    Me, The    91
Lord Who Hears, The    34
Lord Who Sets You
    Apart, The    109
Lord Your Healer, The    70
Man of Pains    44

Merciful God    69
Mighty God    117
Morning Star    110
My Advocate    122
My Beloved    146
My Chosen One    141
My Delight    80
My Deliverer    48
My Helper    68
My Hope    143
My Joy    81
My Portion    134
My Provider—The Lord Will
    See to It    63
My Redeemer    40
My Refuge    66
My Song    85
Our Passover    47
Patient One    86
Pierced One    57
Prince of Peace    45
Prophet, The    147
Real Vine, The    111
Refiner    104
Restorer    138
Resurrection and the Life, The    56

Revealer of Secrets    107
Righteous Servant    58
Righteous Branch    49
Rock, The    135
Root    43
Ruler    15
Searcher of All Hearts    87
Seed of Abraham    53
Shepherd    60
Shield    123
Spirit of Revelation    103
Spirit of the Lord    90
Spirit of Truth    96
Stronghold    128
Teacher    106
The Way, The Truth,
    The Life    105
True and Faithful Witness    137
True God    19
Very Great Reward    142
Warrior    130
Wise God, The    98
Wonder of a Counselor    92
Word, The    100
Your Savior    54